Custom Tools
for
Woodworkers

CUSTOM TOOLS

–for–

WOODWORKERS

*Designing
& making
your own*

Joe Petrovich

Stackpole Books

Copyright © 1990 by Stackpole Books

Published by
STACKPOLE BOOKS
Cameron and Kelker Streets
P.O. Box 1831
Harrisburg, PA 17105

Printed in the United States of America

First Edition

10 9 8 7 6 5 4 3 2 1

Photographs by Richard A. Milewski
Cover design by Tracy Patterson

Library of Congress Cataloging-in-Publication Data
Petrovich, J.
    Custom tools for woodworkers : designing and making your own / J. Petrovich. — 1st ed.
      p. cm.
   ISBN 0-8117-2242-2
    1. Woodworking tools—Design and construction.
  2. Blacksmithing. I. Title.
TT186.P47 1990
682'.4—dc20   89-38450
                       CIP

For Tamberly and Michaela

Contents

Acknowledgments

A book is no easy task and is never really done a cappella. Thank you, friends and colleagues who have been so encouraging and patient over the past year. A special thanks to Dick Milewski, my brother-in-law, whose encouragement and photography grace this book. A respectful thank-you to Dr. John D. Harrison, my father-in-law, whose tutoring in things metallurgic made a good portion of this work possible. A final thank-you to Sally Atwater at Stackpole, whose patience and guidance were above and beyond the call of duty — even for an editor.

Introduction

Toolmaking, contrary to popular belief, is probably the oldest profession. Tools predate art, social organization, language, and probably even fire. The very first evidence of man has been his tools. Tools to this naked, somewhat fragile ape became a means not only to his survival, but also to his success. Tools served as the claws, fangs, horns, and hooves of this less-endowed animal.

Initially tools were only tools of opportunity. The needs of the moment were met by whatever was available. There was little or no refinement to the object at hand. But very early in the evolution of man these tools of opportunity were modified and refined. New methods, new materials, more evolved designs characterized these tools of deliberation. The Old Stone Age proceeded to the New Stone Age and on to the Bronze and Iron ages: the evolution of man is narrated by the evolution of tools.

Toolmaking, as it relates to a particular craft, is as old as that craft itself. As a necessary ancillary to other crafts, toolmaking probably reached its height during the Renaissance and declined thereafter, through the Industrial Revolution. Though industrialization did not kill toolmaking (indeed it is nothing more than another age of man described in terms of his tools), it did so change the nature and character of the craft that tool-making at the individual artisan level all but disappeared—supplanted by the marketplace. Prior to industrialization, artisans typically fashioned their tools based on patterns passed from master to apprentice. Tool-making was an integral *part* of the craft. Tools were not only tools of deliberation, but were also highly personalized, reflecting not only the nature of the craft, but the technique of its user-maker as well. A woodcarver's skew was made to be an expressive extension of his hand and eye. The handle fit his hand. The weight of the shaft balanced the handle. The angle of skew and the cutting angle fit his individual technique. This craftsman knew his tool in a personal and intimate way.

Today there is an enormous array of tools available. Directed toward the needs of the home shop and the small commercial shop, mail-order catalogs offer page after page of romantic photographs depicting the beauty of their tools. With a touch of brass, some rosewood, and a highly polished blade, all of it caught in the drama of muted sidelighting, the humble mortising chisel more closely resembles King Arthur's Excalibur than a tool meant to cut thousands of mortises.

With the abundance of fine tools available in today's market, why would you ever attempt to make your own? Consider for a moment the distinction between tools of opportunity and tools of deliberation. Any mass-manufactured tool is, in a sense, a tool of opportunity—that which is available at the moment. The tool may be well made. It may meet your requirements, fit your hands, your style and technique. It may. That every manufactured tool may meet these requirements is as likely as that a mass-manufactured chair will meet everyone's seating requirements. A mass-manufacturer must aim his product at the largest mass of his market. If he is to be successful, the handle selected for the tool must be generally acceptable — not a perfect fit, but generally acceptable. A tool's heft, its weight and balance, is probably a little heavy for some users or a little light for others. But if the manufacturer is smart and successful, the tool is never too heavy or too light for everyone.

Toolmaking affords the individual craftsman the opportunity to make tools that are not only tools of deliberation in the truest sense, but tools that are highly personalized as well. The handle, the heft, the cutting angle, the hardness, are no longer determined by the generalized requirements of a manufacturer. Based on his own preferences, the craftsman determines and executes the design of his own tool. The result is a degree of artistic and technical control not usually obtained with a mass-manufactured product.

A second consideration in the pursuit of toolmaking is its economy. With practice, familiarity, and a little organization, one can produce high-quality tools economically. The materials are, if one is observant, free or nearly so. The equipment required to produce excellent tools is not necessarily expensive. The greatest initial cost to the beginning toolmaker will be the time spent in learning the craft.

Although it does require time, toolmaking is not a craft that requires years of practice before one obtains any result. Metal, unlike wood, is generally a very predictable material. It demonstrates a reliable consistency that is very reassuring. By following some very basic rules, you can achieve satisfactory results quickly. What produces results with one piece of metal will produce identical results in every other piece of the same type.

Finally, and perhaps most important, toolmaking adds another dimension to your work. With the ability to determine the design of your tools, you tend to look more closely at the *how* of your work. Is the way you work a function of the tools you have on hand? Are there other ways? With your own tools in hand, you develop a sense of ability and capability. You come to realize your own abilities as a craftsman, independent of the limitations imposed by tool manufacturers. You then can establish your own limitations as you match your tools to your work.

1

The Stuff of Steel

Little romance is attached to steel. It is the stuff of boilerplates, bridges, and barbeques. As a material you think of it as rigid and durable—a standard of strength. But there is no romance to it, nothing that you would think of as mysterious. You paint it, coat it, and plate it—not just to protect it, but to make it look like something else.

And yet there was a time, when steel was worked by hand with hammer and anvil, that the metal was shrouded with mystery and magic. Particular types of ore from specific regions were highly prized commodities. Wars were fought for control of those regions. And working the metal—forging, hardening, and tempering—was a highly ritualized, if not religious, process. The men who worked the metal were more like sorcerers or priests than smiths. Extracting the metal was a long and arduous task. "Baking" the material at high and difficult temperatures took days and undoubtedly much incantation. Special powders that the iron was baked with, in fact, produced high-carbon steels. The science was that bone is a good carburizing agent, not that the bone came from the skull of an infidel. Likewise, the quenching baths used to harden red-hot steel read more like recipes from a witch's pharmacopoeia. The science was in the sudden and even cooling of the object and not, as in the case of swords, that it be quenched in the still-living body of an enemy warrior.

Even today a bit of this mystique lingers. We prize and value a tool made of "old steel": "They don't make them out of metal like that anymore," we say. "It held an edge better than any tool I've ever owned." Or, "Grandad gave this chisel to me and it still cuts better than any of those new ones." The truth of such statements probably lies in the strength of your beliefs and consequently in your level of confidence with the tool, rather than in some lost secret of metallurgy. A tool engineered and fabricated from a contemporary steel that has been matched to the purpose will produce a tool more reliably superior than those made at any other time in history. (Admittedly some manufacturers do not exert all the control that they could or should. But then shoddy manufacture is not something new under the sun.)

When I first set out to write this book, my idea was to organize a number of my notes under a general outline and let the book write itself. I'd been making tools for about ten years and had been successful at it. Using Alex Weygers' books *Toolmaking* and *The Modern Blacksmith* (both are excellent resources), I had been designing and making tools for a few years when I took a course from Alex in 1982. Since that time I've made a hundred different tools—most of them successfully. And most of these tools were made as smiths of old made them, with little or no knowledge of metallurgy. Knowing *how* to forge, grind, harden, and temper was generally enough to produce good, usable tools.

Why bother then with describing the *why* of forging, grinding and tempering? In woodworking, you need to know and understand wood when you design a door (there are reasons why solid wood doors have frames and panels); in toolmaking you need to know and understand steel. Similarly, almost anyone can be taught the rudiments of doormaking—of cutting and joining rails and stiles and shaping panels to fit. It is a learnable skill. But presented with a different doorway, the manual skill by itself will fail to provide a solution. The brain needs to know not only how to make the door, but why.

Even though the "why" of steel is fascinating, this overview is brief and bareboned. Much of the theory is left out. Alloys are not covered. The metallurgy covered is applicable to only a limited range of carbon steels (.6 percent to .8 percent carbon). Some terms and processes that have broader application in the field of metallurgy are left unmentioned. Still, despite its limitations, the overview should provide enough explanation for you to begin to understand the process.

A BRIEF METALLURGICAL OVERVIEW
IRON AND CARBON

Quite simply, steel is an alloy of iron and carbon. As with many alloys, steel is more than the sum of its parts. Pure iron is a soft, ductile, and malleable metal very similar to copper. Carbon, in various degrees of purity, is coal, soot, diamond, pencil lead, and burnt lasagna. Together, in the right proportions, they form steel—tough, hard, durable and, most important to your purposes, toolworthy.

The proportion of carbon to iron in forming steel is very slight. Most of the steels suitable for toolmaking are .6 percent to 1.0 percent carbon. A seemingly insignificant amount of carbon (almost nothing more than an impurity level) produces the marvel of steel. Less carbon and the alloy does not have the hardness or durability of tool steel. More carbon and the metal approaches cast iron. And only within this limited range does the alloy respond so dramatically to heat treatment—to hardening and tempering.

The grain, or crystalline structure, of steel is the key to its durability, strength, and flexibility. This crystalline structure, in turn, is determined by the amount of carbon present and by how the steel has been heat-treated. Three pieces of steel of identical chemical composition but different heat-treating may demonstrate entirely different physical properties. One could be so brittle that if dropped, it would shatter. Another could be so workable that it would take and hold a bend. The third piece could be so resilient and flexible that you could bend it into a circle and it would return to its original shape.

The amount of carbon added to steel determines its ultimate obtainable hardness. Generally, the more carbon added (up to .8 percent), the greater the obtainable hardness. As the carbon content rises, however, there is a trade-off: as hardness increases, flexibility decreases. With more than 2 percent carbon it becomes difficult to obtain flexibility. At 3 percent carbon the steel has become cast iron.

As carbon is added to iron, the crystalline structure is changed. At .025 percent carbon, the iron crystals are completely saturated. This saturated state is called *ferrite*. Ferrite, at .025 percent carbon, is a very mild steel, by itself not suitable for tools. As more carbon is added, another type of crystalline structure begins to form. This new substance, *cementite*, at 6.7 percent carbon, is a much harder, though more brittle material. Increasing the carbon content increases the amount of cementite. At .6 percent to 1.0 percent carbon, the amount of cementite formed within the softer ferrite matrix has reached a level that is suitable for tools. There is enough of this harder carbidelike cementite to take and hold an edge, and enough of the softer ferrite to provide a flexible, shock-absorbing matrix.

THE HEAT TREATMENT OF STEEL
HEATING STEEL

Whereas carbon content determines the ultimate *obtainable* hardness (the amount of cementite that could be produced), heat treatment determines the actual hardness and flexibility. How the steel is heated and cooled will determine whether a given piece of steel will shatter, bend, or flex. Heat affects the growth and arrangement of the crystalline structure.

When you heat a carbon steel above 1,340°F (750°C), the softer ferrite matrix and the cementite decompose and recombine to form another substance—*austenite*. Austenite, a form of iron and carbon which exists only at elevated temperatures, will hold up to 2 percent carbon. Depending on how much carbon is in the steel, this austenite transformation will be complete at about 1,450° to 1,650°F (788° to 900°C). When all available carbon has been used up to form austenite, the steel is said to have reached its *critical temperature.*

COOLING THE STEEL

From the critical temperature, you have three distinct processes for cooling the steel. Each results in a distinctly different material.

Annealing. If you cool slowly, over a period of hours, the austenite will gradually transform into a substance called *pearlite.* Not really a new substance per se, pearlite is a physical arrangement of

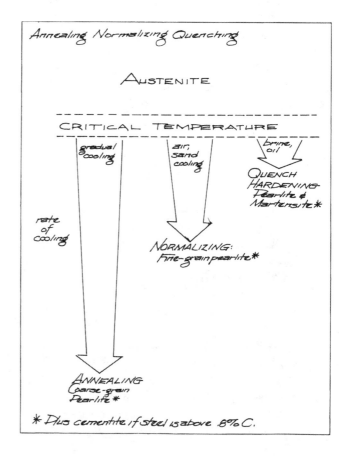

ferrite and cementite in platelets. These platelets begin to form around the austenite crystals as the temperature drops below the critical temperature. Very slow cooling produces a coarse crystalline structure of pearlite. The slower the cooling, the coarser the structure *and* the softer the material. This slow transformation to pearlite is termed *annealing*. This softening of the steel, or annealing, is the result of the hard cementite being surrounded and isolated by the much softer ferrite within the pearlite structure. In this state, the individual cementite crystals have no contiguous network. As such, they are pinpoints of hardness in a sea of ferrite.

It should be noted that the average shop will not be able to fully anneal steel. Full annealing requires thermostatically controlled temperature reduction to encourage the pearlite to grow. Old-timers approached a degree of annealing by burying the object in a bed of coals, allowing it to cool as the fire cooled. For your purposes this partial annealing is sufficient. It reduces a hardened piece of steel to a workable state.

Normalizing. In *normalizing*, the steel is brought up to critical temperature and allowed to cool either in the air or in a sand box. The result is, again, pearlite. In normalizing, however, the crystalline structure is much finer because the cooling is much more rapid. The rapid cooling does not allow the pearlite to grow to any significant size. Because the platelets are smaller, their cementite centers are closer together and therefore produce a material that is harder than the large crystals produced by annealing.

Normalizing has two purposes. In the smaller shop, normalizing is usually a substitute for annealing. Lacking temperature control, you are forced to normalize. The result is a very workable piece of material. The second function of normalizing is to prepare the steel for forging or hardening.

A piece of steel in a fully annealed condition has a coarse pearlite structure. This structure is not only soft, but it is frequently weak as well. If the structure size is not reduced before you work the material, as in forging or bending, the material may fail. After forging, particularly heavy forging, even a fine pearlite structure may be severely stressed. The internal structure may be stretched, compressed, and bent as a result of shaping the steel. Normalizing will relieve these stresses. It is a good practice to normalize after forging is complete and before the next cooling process: quench-hardening.

Quench-hardening. In both annealing and normalizing, the intent is to soften the steel. *Quenching* has the opposite effect. As in annealing and normalizing, the steel is brought to its critical temperature. Instead of cooling slowly, however, the steel is quenched in a brine or oil bath. This accelerated cooling results in a different transformation. Where slow cooling resulted in pearlite, rapid cooling results in *martensite.* The austenite transformation, which is complete at the critical temperature, cannot shed itself of carbon quickly enough to begin forming pearlite. The result is a sort of quick-frozen ferrite that is supersaturated with carbon. (Remember, ferrite is normally .025 percent carbon.) In this high-carbon state, the material is much harder than pearlite or ferrite. If the process has been done properly, the material is said to be *fully hardened.* In this fully hardened state, the material is also very brittle. Thinner sections, if dropped, are liable to shatter.

In quench-hardening, not all of the steel is transformed to martensite (unless the material is quite thin). Because the core of the object still cools relatively slowly, it is transformed into pearlite. The thickness of the martensite around the pearlite core is termed the *depth of case.* Obviously, this depth of case needs to be deep enough that the working part of the tool (usually the cutting edge) is included in the hardening process. While depth of case can be controlled metallurgically with alloys, this is not a likely course of action for the average shop. Good quenching techniques, however, can maximize depth of case.

Now, in considering the transformation to martensite, it would seem that the quicker the quench, the deeper the case. Ideally, then, one would use a very cold liquid. Unfortunately, the hardening process is not that straightforward. The formation of martensite is a very stressful process. Sudden volume changes and a number of other internal stresses make the process almost violent. If the bath is too cool, the steel will not survive this internal violence. For this reason the quench bath is normally kept at room temperature.

The quenching medium is equally important. Most tools can be successfully quenched in brine (a 10 percent solution of salt to water). Brine is used because it has a higher boiling point than water. A piece of steel at 1,650°F (924°C) will heat the brine immediately surrounding it to its vapor point. An envelope of vapor will surround the object. In plain water the temperature of this vapor will be around 212°F (119°C) before it bubbles away. In brine, the temperature at which it boils away is 30°F (17°C) higher.

How the object is immersed in the quenching medium is also important. Imagine the object with this envelope of vapor surrounding it; you can continually break through the envelope with a stirring motion. By stirring, the object can always be touching "fresh," unvaporized medium. If the stirring motion is regular, one portion of the object will be cooled more than another. An irregular motion will help to even the cooling and therefore the depth of case.

Not all objects can be quenched in brine. Objects that are thin in cross section, say 3/16 inch (5 mm) or less, present a number of problems. First of all, the material may harden all the way through the object. If this is done in brine, the violence may be too thorough for the object to remain intact. Second, if there is no core of pearlite to maintain the shape, the cooling will have to be exactly equal, or the object will distort, shrinking more on one side that the other. For these thinner objects, a quenching medium of oil is used (motor oil, olive oil, animal fat). Oil has a much higher boiling point than brine. The temperature of the vapor envelope surrounding the object is therefore higher than it would be if the object were quenched in brine. The depth of case is not as great, but the violence has been reduced. Distortion and rupture are avoided.

Full hardening leaves most edge tools too brittle for general use. The martensite, though hard, is tense, stressed, and generally unstable. Because the martensite is not a stable state for steel, the carbon can be coaxed out of the martensite with relatively little heat to form a fine, even structure of ferrite and cementite. There is, of course, a trade-off in this process. The hardness of martensite is traded for the toughness of the ferrite and cementite.

Tempering. This trade-off is controllable. The less heat applied, the less this transformation occurs. Controlling the heat controls the hardness. The process of controlling the hardness is called *tempering*. Just as the color of heat will indicate having reached the steel's critical temperature, there are surface colors (oxidization, actually) that appear in sequence when tempering.

While this sounds easy enough, tempering requires skill and patience. First of all, tools generally have a variety of dimensions. Heating thicker parts of the tool will build a reservoir of heat that, when it flows to a thinner section, will overflow and overheat the metal.

Second, in order to assure a thorough tempering, the temperature of the steel needs to be maintained for ten to fifteen minutes. The tempering colors indicate only the attainment of a temperature, and not its maintenance. A short, high burst of temperature may produce the appropriate color on the outside without effecting any significant transformation inside. Likewise, bringing the object up to the proper color quickly and then quenching to stop the transformation does not provide for thorough tempering.

While industry uses thermostatically controlled ovens, the average shop can make do with a propane torch or a gas range. By varying the distance from the flame and keeping the tool in motion — lingering over thicker sections, and moving more quickly over thinner sections — one develops a technique that provides a deep and even temper.

Tempering also allows for some degree of "metallurgical engineering." Different parts of the tool require greater degrees of hardness (such as cutting edges) while other parts (shafts, tangs) require more toughness. Careful and selective tempering can provide this degree of engineering.

A TYPICAL PROCEDURE

Given a brief metallurgical understanding of how and why steel behaves as it does, you need to apply your understanding to a procedure to make it practical. Beginning with a piece of steel of unknown composition, you'll follow a procedure that will take you from identification through the final phase of tempering. Along the way you'll take a look at the metallurgy or the "why" of what you're doing. Understanding the "why" should make remembering the "how" a lot easier.

IDENTIFICATION

Before you invest time and energy in working up a piece of steel, you need to verify that it is a *carbon steel*. If there is low carbon or no carbon, there is no hardening, no tempering, no tool. Probably the easiest way to identify suitable carbon content in stccl is with the spark test. Steel, when held to a rotating grinding wheel, will spark. Thc heat of abrasion causes the fine particles of steel being removed to burn. Fortunately, the sparks vary for steels of differing compositions. Steel that is in the carbon range that you are looking for sparks a light yellow-orange, and the sparks themselves burst, or "star". Steel that is too low in carbon for your purposes sparks a dull orange and has few stars.

To make the comparison more vivid, take an old file and a lag screw. Held to the grinder, the old file, at around .75 percent carbon, will spark brilliantly with many separate stars. The lag screw, at around .2 percent to .3 percent carbon, will be dull and have few, if any, bursts.

Not all of the materials you test will fit into one of these categories. Some will have the spark pattern generally correct, but the color will be reddish, and perhaps the sparks themselves will be thinner—still bursting, but thinner. These materials are probably alloys and not simply carbon steel. Heat-treating these alloy steels would be a matter of guesswork for the individual toolmaker. The different treatment temperatures for these steels vary greatly, according to the alloying material and its quantity. Some alloying materials have very high critical temperatures. Some are easily ruined by overheating. Some require special quenching techniques, and others are air quenched. In almost all

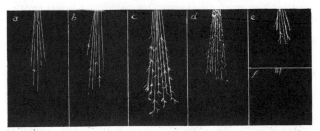

Spark Test: **a,** Slight sparking iron; **b,** Few sparks indicate mild steel; **c,** Many bright, strong sparks indicate carbon steel; **d, e, f,** Various alloyed steels.

cases, they will not respond to the treatment described here. Unless you happen to buy steel from a supply house and have the treatment instructions provided, it is best to avoid these alloy steels.

A second method of identifying many steels is by the form that it is currently in. Auto springs (both coil and leaf), files, old saw blades (large commercial band saws, old lumber mill saws, and old circular saw blades) all indicate excellent sources of steel. In most instances, the material can be had for little or nothing. (One item to be avoided that sometimes passes the spark test is concrete reinforcing rod, more commonly known as re-bar. As a result of its manufacture, re-bar may have pockets of carbon steel, but it is generally untrustworthy.)

GRINDING

If your tool is to be mostly a grinding exercise (no forging), like a small knife or a flat-bladed screwdriver, normalize the material before you begin grinding. Transforming the material into pearlite before grinding has two advantages. First of all, the stock will be easier to grind. Remember, pearlite is much softer than a ferrite/cementite structure. Second, the softer material is easier on the grinder. Grinding the teeth off of an old file that has not been normalized or annealed can be hard and time-consuming work.

Grinding may also be a preparation for forging. For the beginner, the slower pace of grinding may save time later when forging. Some objects must be ground before forging or heat-treating. Files, for example, must have their teeth removed before forging lest the teeth fold over one another. Likewise, file teeth are liable to establish cracks in the object during heat-treating. For other objects it is sometimes helpful to chamfer edges with the grinder so that folding does not occur.

A final note on grinding. It is entirely possible to overheat steel when grinding. Normalizing the steel does not protect it from overheating. Steel can be burned on even a small grinder. Go slowly.

FORGING

Now that you've verified your material as a usable carbon steel and you've removed the sharp edges at the grinder, you're ready to begin forging. If you do not know anything about the material that you're working, except that it passed the spark test, and you haven't normalized the steel, you should do so now. I do it as a matter of habit. That first heat allows me to adjust my eyes to colors I'll be looking for and gives me an idea of how long a heat will take.

More tools are ruined in forging than in any other procedure. The most common error is that of not reading or ignoring the color of heat. Forging temperature begins at about 900°F (480°C). This is the first appearance in the visible spectrum of the color of heat. Actually, the safe forging temperature is above 1,700°F (952°C) and below 1,900°F (1,064°C). As steel is in a relatively plastic state at these temperatures, it can be moved quite dramatically without fear of cracking. As the temperature drops below this range, the steel again becomes more and more rigid. While steel may be bent or twisted slightly at these lower temperatures, it resists the suddenness of hammer forging. Therefore, it is generally safe to make minor corrections down to about 900°F (480°C). Again, these are *minor* corrections: straightening a shaft, aligning a blade, making a gentle bend. For someone caught in the rush and excitement of forging, it is easy to forget the color. Striking the steel after it has dipped below the forging temperature may crack or even break the forging. Even though the steel has been normalized during the forging (heated to above its critical temperature and allowed to cool in the air), forging itself sets up stresses in the steel. The pearlite may be twisted, compressed, and elongated in a very small space as a result of forging. A hammer

Temperature and Color of Steel During Tempering, Forging, and Hardening		
F	**C**	**Color**
100°	37.8°	
200	93	
300	149	
400	204	428°F: Beginning of tempering colors (pale yellow).
500	260	
600	316	610°F: End of tempering colors (pale blue).
700	371	
800	427	No color — Only gentle, minor movements.
900	482	Faint red — Forging range begins.
1000	538	
1050	566	Blood red
1075	580	Dark cherry
1100	593	
1200	649	
1250	677	Medium cherry
1300	704	1340°F: Austenite begins to form.
1375	746	Cherry
1400	760	1414°F: Loss of magnetic properties.
1500	816	End of forging range. Beginning of hardening range.
1550	843	Light cherry — End of hardening range. Annealing temperature.
1600	871	
1650	899	Salmon — 1670°F: Austenite transformation complete. Beginning of safe forging range.
1700	927	
1725	940	Orange
1800	982	
1825	996	Lemon
1900	1038	
1975	1079	Light yellow — End of safe forging range.
2000	1093	
2100	1149	
2200	1204	White
2300	1260	
2350	1288	Dazzling white — Steel begins to spark and burn.

blow made below forging temperature along a stressed area may be enough to cause breakage. Sometimes worse than an obvious breakage is a small crack that, covered by the scale of the fire, remains undetected until grinding or polishing.

The second major error in forging is overheating. As the steel exceeds its critical temperature, there are a number of potential problems. First of all, the austenite crystals will continue to grow in size. If you recall that the pearlite is formed from the edges of the austenite crystals, this overheating may establish a crystalline structure that is not only coarse but uneven as well. The steel is in a significantly weakened condition and subject to breakage. Normalizing will, however, correct this condition. The coarse pearlite will dissolve into a fine austenite structure if kept at the critical temperature. Air cooling will produce a finer pearlite structure from this finer austenite structure.

Overheating can also cause a reduction in the carbon content. The greater the overheat, the greater the carbon loss.

The ultimate overheat is displayed as a dazzling or sparkling white that occurs when steel actually burns. There is no cure for burned steel. The burned area must be thoroughly removed. Depending on the size of the area burned and the amount of time that you have invested in the tool, you may want to begin again. What happens to steel at these temperatures is a very rapid oxidization. Somewhat like a violent rusting process, burning does not leave the steel intact. It is not just a crystalline change. The steel has been *chemically* changed. It is no longer steel.

In addition to shaping steel, forging has a secondary purpose for some steels. It serves as a mixer. Cementite tends to form a network each time the steel enters the austenite phase. This network, if allowed to grow, becomes a network of brittleness throughout the tool. Forging breaks up this network and mechanically distributes the cementite.

The final step in forging is to normalize. Again, the grinding that follows will be easier, and normalizing will remove the stresses developed during forging.

REFINING THE SHAPE

A handforged tool is generally not ready for hardening immediately after forging. Some refinement is necessary. Depending on your standards and the eventual use of the tool, a lot of refinement may be necessary. Forging leaves hammermarks, scale, and an occasional pockmark if the fire is unclean. To remove the blemishes, you'll grind, sand, and polish.

While the risk here is burning the steel, just as it was in the initial grinding, the purpose now is to shape and smooth the steel. The smoother the surface and the closer to final shape that you get it at this stage, the less work required after hardening.

The exception is the cutting edge; it should be only roughly established, if at all. Unless it is a thick blade, $3/16$ inch (5 mm) or more, leave the edge blunt. This is done, first of all, because thin sections — especially cutting thin — will burn during hardening, and this reduces tool size. Secondly, a very thin section may transform completely to martensite. If this edge is of any size, it may distort or, if it can't distort because the rest of the tool is too massive to be moved, it may crack instead. Quenching in oil might save the cutting edge, but it probably would not harden the rest of the tool satisfactorily. At this stage you want to avoid creating too thin a section.

Just as in preparing a wood surface for finishing, this part of your grinding is done with finer and finer abrasives. Though abrasives and grinding techniques will be covered later, it is important to note here that you need a smooth, if not polished, surface when you are done refining. Refining ought to be considered a preparation to the next phase, hardening. By smoothing the steel now, removing its pits and irregularities while it is in a relatively soft condition, you save time, energy, and abrasives later.

HARDENING

At this point you've shaped, refined, and polished the tool; it has literally taken shape in your hands. You've taken what was probably a scrap of steel and transformed it with hammer, anvil, stone, and sweat into what is now almost a tool. It has the line, the heft, and the feel of a tool. And now, out of what can seem more ritual than science (and what once *was* more ritual than science), you'll put that almost-a-tool back into the fire until it glows a light cherry red. Then, trusting in your eyes to recognize the color of the heat, you'll take that glowing steel — at just the right moment — and plunge it into a bath that will hiss, bubble, and steam. It is easy to share the sense of magic your ancient brethren saw in the process. Without the science of it, it seems more like an offering to some god of fire and forge. The science of it is, quite simply, the transformation of austenite to martensite.

Before hardening, the steel is a fine, even pearlite. If you were reasonably cautious during your grinding and polishing, you have done nothing to change that. Pearlite is much too soft for a tool. It would never hold an edge. Frequent resharpenings would quickly use it up.

In hardening, you'll heat the tool to its critical temperature, at which point it will be transformed into austenite. When you quench, the austenite will be transformed to some depth (depth of case) to martensite — that quick-frozen ferrite that is supersaturated with carbon. You are reducing the steel's temperature in a matter of seconds by 1,600°F (896°C). Like any self-respecting substance, the steel is severely put upon to remain intact. What with volume changes and unstable molecular arrangements, the steel almost hums with tension and stress.

Your task as a toolmaker is, if not to minimize the stress, at least to balance it. You balance these stresses by selecting the appropriate quenching medium and by matching your quenching technique to the size and shape of the tool.

Brine. Brine is both the easiest and the safest of the quenching media. It produces the greatest depth of case as well. Unfortunately, brine also produces the most stress in the object being quenched. For this reason, you should use brine only for thicker tools—those that are greater than ³/₁₆ inch (5 mm) in section. Because the tool is thick, during the quench not all of the tool is transformed to martensite. The core of the tool, because it cools more slowly, will be a fine, even pearlite. This pearlite core will help resist the tendency to distort. Likewise, to balance the stresses of one side of the tool against the other (and to cool as quickly as possible), you stir the tool in an irregular motion. Irregular stirring will break through that envelope of vapor that forms instantly around the tool during the quench. (Simply stirring in a circle allows the side facing the direction of stir to escape the vapor envelope while the opposing side does not until halfway through the stir. Depending on how vigorously you stir, this difference in cooling times could result in distortion.)

For most of the thicker tools, a brine solution and irregular stirring will produce a satisfactory result. The pearlite core and the even hardening will provide the necessary balance to a successful quench. There are exceptions, however.

Consider for a moment a broad, flat object such as a drawknife. Even if it is greater than ³/₁₆ inch (5 mm) in section, you need to concern yourself with the balance of hardening one side against the other. Both the depth of case and the timing of the hardening need to be the same for both sides. If one side has a greater depth of case than the other, the tool may cup around it. If one side is cooled more quickly than the other, even though each hardens to the same depth, a warp may result before the other side can resist it. In either event, the result is unsatisfactory — a distorted or cracked tool.

To counteract this imbalance when quenching tools that have broad, flat, opposing surfaces, the tool should be immersed edgewise into the brine. This will cause the cooling to be simultaneous. Instead of stirring, move the tool up and down edgewise in the brine. While this may not provide as great a depth of case as stirring would, it will balance the process and avoid distortion.

Which edge should enter first? The thick edge. Again, it is a matter of balance. Even though you haven't ground a cutting edge yet, you have probably reduced the thickness of what will be the cutting edge. Because this edge is thinner and its sides are not parallel, quenching evenly can be a problem.

Oil. Many of your tools will be thinner than 3/16 inch (5 mm). Quenching these tools in brine is generally too violent. Without a sufficient, resistant core of pearlite, the tool is highly subject to distortion, cracking, or even breakage. For this reason, thinner sections are quenched in oil. Oil has a higher boiling point than water, so when quenching, the vapor envelope is a higher temperature. This slows the transformation significantly. Additionally, since oil is more viscous than brine, the envelope of vapor escapes more slowly and so removes the heat less quickly.

For thinner sections, this slowing of the hardening process results in much less stress. Although the depth of case is reduced because the cooling is slower, it's not a concern because the tool itself is thinner. Unfortunately, an oil quench does not guarantee success. Just as in the brine quench, where broad faces oppose one another, the edgewise technique of quenching will balance the hardening. In other shapes, a general rule of thumb is to quench the thicker sections first, but as much of the tool at the same time as is possible.

What kind of oil? For your purposes, motor oil is satisfactory. There is, however, a vast pharmacopoeia of suitable quenching oils. From commercially produced mixtures to animal fat (particularly sheep renderings) and olive oil, toolmakers, after a time, find their own favorite. Whatever the choice of oil, it needs to be in a sturdy, lidded metal container. (Plastic pails are dangerous. A tool at 1,650°F (924°C) will burn through the plastic almost instantly.) The vapor in the envelope that eventually bubbles to the surface may still be at its flash point. If it is ignited by the tool, the oil will burn. It is not an explosion, but it *is* a situation that needs control. **Water is not the solution.** Placing the lid back onto the container will smother the fire.

TEMPERING

Finishing. After hardening, the steel has lost its shine but, ideally, not its shape. If the tool did distort, take it back to the forge, reheat, correct the distortion, and reharden. Even a small distortion after hardening is not correctable without reheating. If your fire was clean, the discoloration is superficial and easily removed. If the fire was not so clean, there may be some mill scale, or in the worst case, even some pitting. In any event, the tool must be clean and polished before tempering.

This final polishing is more than cosmetic. A smooth surface is easier to "read" during the tempering process. Because the temper colors are an oxidization process, the surface needs to be clean as well as polished. Any surface contamination may interfere with the oxidization and so give a false indication. After polishing, wash the tool. Hot soapy water will remove most polishing compound residues. (Alcohol, acetone, and MEK also work well and are sometimes more convenient in the shop. Be certain to remove these flammables, however, before lighting your heat source.) Once you have washed or swabbed the tool with a solvent, do not handle the tool. In its clean, pristine state, even fingerprints can blemish the surface. For this reason, save the final cleaning until just before you're ready to temper. If there is a lapse of a day or two between final polish and tempering, leave the residue on the tool to protect it from rust.

Heat source. The temperatures required to temper are well below the forging range. In the 400°F to 600°F (224°C to 336°C) range there are a number of suitable heat sources: the kitchen stove; a gas, propane, or acetylene torch; the forge; even the kitchen oven, if the thermocouple is accurate. Toolmakers adjust their techniques to their sources.

The colors. The colors of tempering are striking. Reproducing them in pigment does not do them justice. They have a quality of depth and iridescence that must be seen to be recognized and appreciated. The different colors are the colors of surface oxidization at particular temperatures. They are a visible indication that the fully hardened tool (its martensite case) is being transformed by increments to ferrite and cementite. By controlling the degree or amount of martensite being transformed, you control the trade-off between hardness and toughness. Each color is an indication that the temperature at which this increment of change occurs has been reached. This is important to understand. *The colors do not indicate the actual change.* They indicate that the temperature at which the change occurs has been obtained. Unlike the martensite transformation, which is nearly instantaneous, tempering requires a period of maintenance at the correct temperature (five to ten minutes). Commercial operations use thermostatically controlled ovens to insure a thorough tempering. That is why tempering by hand and eye is a relatively slow and conservative process. If one could rely on the colors to indicate the actual transformation, it would be relatively easy to heat quickly to the appropriate color and quench. This is, unfortunately, not the case.

Technique. Tempering ought to be a slow process of patient observation. Even though the tool is almost finished, this is not the time to rush things. The heat needs to penetrate the tool evenly, gradually, controllably. As the tool's temperature rises, the colors begin to appear: first a barely discernible pale straw, which darkens through bronze and brown to peacock, purple, and blue. Because the temperature differences between these colors are slight, they can easily go too far too fast. To overheat now means going back to rehardening, recleaning and repolishing.

While tempering by hand and eye has some drawbacks (it is dependent upon skill, and skill implies some risk), it also has some distinct advantages. It allows you to engineer the tool — to make one part harder and more rigid and to make other parts softer, more shock-absorbing. Take a minute or two to think about the tool — about how it ought to behave. The cutting edge ought to be hard, more resistant to wear. The shaft and tang ought to be more flexible than hard. For the cutting edge, a straw temper color will leave the steel hard enough to maintain an edge yet tough enough to resist cracking or chipping under pressure. For the shaft of the tool, a purple or blue will provide the flexibility and shock absorption it needs. How to get there requires a little thinking.

The shaft of the tool is probably thicker than the rest of the tool. It will require more heat to get to purple than the cutting edge will require to get to straw. If you heat the shaft first, you'll load this thicker section with heat, which will naturally transfer to the thinner, cooler section. If all balances well (the thickness and thinness of sections), the tool almost tempers itself while you watch. Or so it would seem. Actually, your only control over the process — your means for insuring the balance — is the amount of heat applied. Controlling the amount of heat is a matter of practice and patience.

I use a propane torch for tempering. It has a variety of nozzle attachments that allow control of the shape and size of the flame. Holding the tool 8 to 10 inches (200 to 250 mm) above a low flame, move the tool back and forth in slow, even strokes (about as fast as petting a napping dog). To insure even heating, rotate the tool, exposing a different side to the heat with each stroke. Initially, you should heat the entire tool using the stroke-and-rotate method. At this point, you are not after color; in fact, you don't want color. What you are doing is raising the temperature of the entire tool so that one part is not markedly cooler than the other part. Heat transfer is always in the direction of the cooler material. By gradually and evenly heating the entire tool, you have a starting point where the whole tool is just about to turn color. Apply a little more heat and the tool will change color. By heating the whole tool in this manner, there is a visible and direct relationship between speed of your stroke and the colors appearing. This reduces the chances of building a large reservoir of heat in the shaft that suddenly runs out to a cold cutting edge. In short, you have control.

Having elevated the temperature of the whole tool evenly, you can now focus on the thicker sections. Heat control is the key. Given an open flame, there are really only two methods of heat control available: distance from the flame and duration over the flame. Distance is probably the most difficult to judge. How much greater is the heat if you move it 2 inches (50 mm) closer? And if you move it 3 inches (80 mm) closer? If you make the distance a constant, that is, if you maintain the same distance between the flame and the tool, you can increase the heat by slowing the stroke gradually.

If the tool does not respond, don't stop your stroke or lower the tool to catch up; there probably was not a sufficient initial heating. Continue to work just the thicker section. But be observant — that first sign of straw coloring is very subtle. Once the straw begins to appear, observe how far it runs. If it moves down to the cutting edge, shift your heating away from the edge. This is as far as you need to temper the edge. Focus on the shaft. Heat nearer the tang, and leave a buffer area between the shaft and the cutting edge. This buffer will act as a safety to allow heat to move toward the edge (you hope) without overrunning it.

Some general suggestions on tempering:

• Tempering takes time. It may take five minutes before any color appears.

• Be comfortable. Set up the torch so that you can move the tool back and forth without fatigue or discomfort.

• Observe. The colors that appear blend very quickly sometimes. Bronze, peacock, and blue can be very difficult to distinguish from one another. And that first appearance of straw color can seem like it will never come and then suddenly pass by. Keep a piece of polished, untempered steel handy for comparison.

• Practice. Before trying it on a tool, temper a scrap piece a few times. Get a feel for the colors and the speed at which they appear and blend.

• Be patient. Patience is necessary not only to the process, but to learning the process as well.

2

Equipment

There are blacksmiths throughout the world who, with very limited resources and equipment, produce exquisite forgings. I have seen a smith in a small village (equipped with an open-pit charcoal fire, a primitive set of portable bellows, a reclaimed piece of cast iron for an anvil, two hammers, and two files) forge and hammer-weld a new plowpoint. This man, however, had been doing this work all his life—from an apprenticeship with his father and grandfather to that point in time, fifty years later, when I met him in the central highlands of Viet Nam.

I have also visited a number of American blacksmiths, knifemakers, and toolmakers. Their shops reflect, in many instances, an entire epoch in technological advances: grinders, lathes, mills, heat-treating furnaces, even hardness testers. These are men, too, who produce exquisite work.

What I suggest for a starting point, a place to begin making your own tools, lies somewhere between these two extremes. A great deal of creative, useful work can be done in a very limited space with a minimum of equipment.

THE SPACE

Most of you have a work area or shop. Unfortunately, metalworking is generally less than compatible with woodworking. Forging, grinding, and torchwork all produce dirt that finds its way into everything—including your woodwork. The heat and sparks produced are potentially dangerous. What's more, metalworking moves at a rhythm that is quite different from that of woodworking. The work is slower but more violent. The area of focus is more limited, the tolerances tighter. The medium itself, the steel, is more rigid, more exacting, less forgiving. Toolmaking requires a different frame of mind than the work you do in your woodshop.

A place to work, however, need not be an elaborate affair. Despite all the inconveniences, for more than ten years my toolmaking was done in my woodshop. I would set up my forge in the backyard, do the rough forging outside, and bring the rough forgings into the shop. Inside, I did the finish work — the grinding, the filing, the sanding, and the polishing. After the finish work, it was back outside to the forge to harden. After hardening, it was back inside to repolish, temper, and put a handle on the tool. The back and forth, the cleaning required to make the shop safe from fires, the cleanup necessary to keep the metal dust out of the woodwork, setting up and stowing away the forge and the anvil — all of it was not as difficult as it seems now . . . now that I have a separate shop.

Whether you have the opportunity for a separate shop or must deal with an available space, here are some variables that you must consider.

LIGHTING

Indoor space for grinding, filing, and polishing requires good lighting. Fluorescent lights are economical — both in the initial outlay for the fixtures and bulbs, and in the amount of power consumed during use. Incandescent fixtures, particularly the inexpensive clamp-on variety, make excellent supplemental fixtures. Although the fluorescents provide good overall lighting, the incandescents can be used more directly to focus light on a specific worksite. Incandescents are also handy for side lighting — for detecting surface irregularities. And when forced to temper tools at night, I prefer the quality of incandescent light to pick out the temper colors as they appear. At the low end of the tempering spectrum, light straw seems difficult to spot as it first appears under fluorescent light.

VENTILATION

Most of us have small shops. Part of the basement, the garage, or perhaps a small outbuilding is about all we can afford. In these small areas, there is seldom adequate ventilation. Ideally, each machine would be vented to a vacuum system. Vented hoods would remove the vapors. Air filters would clean the air and recirculate it. In most instances, however, the space and budget available rule out this ideal. What to do?

First of all, vent wherever you can. Open the windows and doors. Installing an exhaust fan is a good idea, but even a small table fan will help. Direct it at an angle out the door or window and it will help start circulation.

Second, there are face masks. I detest them. They never seal properly around my more-than-adequate nose and so my glasses fog. If you are bearded, the seal is even poorer. Still, for most of us, masks are the only sure protection short of abstinence. Be certain that the mask fits the task. Some are rated for particulates only. Others filter out fumes and are so labeled. I use this latter variety only for fumes. The usually replaceable filters on the fume-rated masks load quickly with particles, so it is more economical to save them just for fume protection.

A final note on masks: Buy one that you will wear. Medical science seems to discover a new carcinogen every month. Until you can afford a properly vented shop, the mask is your only protection.

FLOORS

For most woodshops, a wooden floor is a luxury. Wooden floors are easier on the legs and feet and warmer in the winter than a concrete floor. Unfortunately, wooden floors are much more sensitive to fire. If you have a choice, a concrete floor is superior for metalwork. It is not only fireproof, but it is also easier to maintain than a wooden floor. The metal dust and hot workpieces that find their way to the floor do not damage concrete.

OUTDOOR SPACE

Forgework really belongs outdoors. The heat generated by a forge in a limited space would make the shop unpleasant at the very least. The smoke, should you start the forge without a hood and vent, would make the shop unbearable. You will find, too, that it is nice to be able to stand away from the forge occasionally, remove your mask, and breathe some fresh air.

The outdoor space obviously should be located away from combustible materials. It should also offer as little offense to your neighbors as possible. Although the forge will smoke only when first lit, that initial cloud may dampen your neighbors' en-

Lay out your shop for efficiency so that nothing is more than a step away. Clockwise from upper left: foot-operated, oil quench bucket; 30-gallon wooden quench barrel; forge; 5-gallon water bucket; leg vise; hammer rack; 150-pound anvil.

thusiasm for your new avocation. Generally speaking, a forge is not going to present any more danger than a barbeque. Common sense is sufficient to make forge operation safe.

If you plan to build a structure for your forge and equipment, experiment before anything is committed to concrete. We all have different work habits. I prefer the anvil, forge, water barrel, hammers, tongs, and vise all very close. In fact, it is difficult for two people to work at my forge. I like knowing where everything is and having it no more than an arm's length away. The layout in the illustration shows how I have set up my forge area. But again, before you commit to a setup, experiment in the backyard. Discover what will work for you.

FORGING EQUIPMENT

Not all toolmaking requires a forge. In fact, most tools can be made by removing material rather than forging it. Many of the tools in this book are made by cutting and grinding what was already a piece of forgework into the appropriate shape. Chisels, plane irons, screwdrivers, and awls can all be designed to be made by grinding. Knives, too, can be made without a forge—though many say that a forged edge is superior to a purely ground edge. Even the gouge can be made by grinding.

Why bother with forging? Why invest time, money, and energy in a forge? The answer is, quite simply, versatility. Grinding, or the wasting process (removing material rather than modeling it), requires that the blank have the major dimensions of the finished tool prior to grinding. In many instances this is no real problem. Flat, straight-sided tools, such as plane irons, screwdrivers, and knives, can all be cut from a multitude of sources—discarded saw blades, old files, worn-out planer blades, and auto leaf springs. It is relatively easy to cut these as wide silhouettes and grind to the scribed line.

Other tools—those that must be made round or oval in cross section or, by virtue of their size or use require major dimensional changes and bends—are better and more quickly done at the forge. Tools such as the mortising chisel, the slick, and the gouge are, in fact, quite difficult to make without the forge. The forge allows you to build up, reduce, bend, and straighten the steel blank quickly and efficiently. With very little practice it is possible to produce forgings that require only minor touch-up work at the grinder.

Not only does the forge reduce grinding to a process of refinement, it also allows for a wider range of material selection. Because in forging the steel is modeled, you are no longer limited to material of a specific dimension. The steel can be shaped or molded much as a sculptor works in clay. Forging expands your resources to include automobile coil springs, garage door springs, drive shafts, axles, and a multitude of other scrap steel that lies quietly rusting in backyards, alleys, and roadsides. In our replace-rather-than-repair society there will probably always be a surfeit of material for those willing to salvage it.

Forging is fast. Most tools require much less than an hour at the forge—even for beginners. As your abilities increase, your speed will increase. With this increased speed comes the confidence to manage several "irons in the fire" at the same time. By contrast, grinding tools from a blank, especially tools with a variety of cross sections, requires a great deal of time and considerable practice.

Finally, I prefer to forge tools because the method is more direct. Michelangelo spoke of seeing his sculptures in the marble and merely removing the material that surrounded them. I would have to look long and hard to find a piece of steel that even suggested a gouge or a cranked neck. It is more direct to move the steel into the shape. As I work, the tool takes shape, emerges, and evolves—and not necessarily according to plan. Perhaps the emerging tool seems too heavy and clumsy for its purpose. I can thin it out, refine it. Perhaps the bend in the shaft is not quite right. It can be modified. The whole process of shaping the tool is then one of question and response, question and response . . . a sort of fluid dialogue. And when the moment is just right, when all the angles are comfortable and the axes in line, when the heft and feel of the blank seem perfect, at that moment it can all be frozen precisely in place. Such is the substance of forging.

BUILDING A FORGE

The forge, though it is an important piece of equipment, need not be expensive. I have seen and used car wheels, truck wheels, even barbeques converted into forges. And though the heating area was somewhat limited, they were generally satisfactory for forging tools.

Systematically, a forge is quite simple. A *tuyere* (pronounced "to yeah") provides a directed stream of air to the coal burning in the firepot. The in-

A short-legged farrier's forge powered by a commercial blower. All this equipment was found at flea markets.

creased volume of air causes the coal to oxidize, or burn more rapidly, thus increasing the amount of heat produced. The amount of energy in a given quantity of coal is fixed. If it is forced to burn hotter, the length of time it will burn is reduced.

Let's look at the systematic diagram of the forge. Unfortunately, nothing is ever as easy as systems analysis would lead us to believe. Depending on the air source's capabilities, and how much and how well the coal is arranged, the temperatures at the heart of the fire may exceed 2,500°F (1,400°C). If the firepot were nothing more than sheet metal, as in a barbeque, the fire would burn its way through. Moreover, an air source directly below the firepot permits hot ash and embers to fall down the tuyere and damage the air source. To improve the system, a few design changes are necessary. Lining the firepot with refractory cement insulates and protects the metal shell of the firepot. A metal grate with holes of about ¼ to ⅜ inch (6 to 10 mm) keeps the larger embers from falling down the tuyere. Installing the air source at the side of the tuyere lessens the possibility of damage by hot ash and embers to the source. Finally, an ash bin or trap provides a means of removing the debris that would accumulate in the tuyere.

Although old forges in reparable condition can sometimes be found, it is not difficult to fabricate a usable system. The firepot and tuyere are easy to find. The grate is a little more difficult. I have seen old urinal and shower grates used. (Be sure that whatever you use is not brass or aluminum because neither will withstand the heat.) If your search through junkyards and garage sales fails, you can make your own. Use ¼- to ⅜-inch (6- to 10-mm) mild steel. Drill it first with ¼- to ⅜-inch (6- to 10-mm) holes. Heat the grate with whatever you have available—a torch, another forge, or you can even try heating it in a barbeque enhanced with a hair dryer. Forge the grate into a dome shape by using the ball end of your largest ball peen hammer

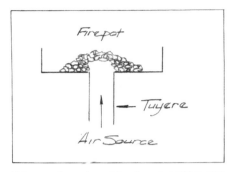

From a systems viewpoint, a forge is nothing more than a firepot that provides for oxygen-enriched combustion.

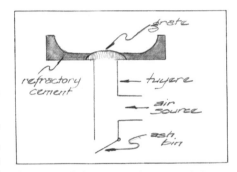

From a practical standpoint, the systematic forge needs some modification due to the requirements of coal as a fuel.

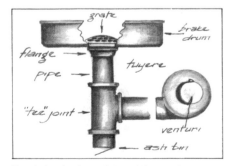

Translating the theory into practice requires some innovation. A forge can be constructed from a number of commonplace items.

striking at the center of the steel in gradually widening concentric circles. The edges of the disc will
gradually rise. A ½- to ¾-inch (13- to 19-mm) rise
will produce a dome sufficient to properly disperse
the air. If the holes enlarge during the forging process, it will not ruin the grate. You should be able to
adjust the amount of air at the blower, so the holes
can be enlarged up to about ½ inch (13 mm) without impairing the grate's effectiveness.

For an air source, an old vacuum cleaner, clothes
dryer motor and cage, or even a heavy-duty hair
dryer will provide enough air to do the job—in
some cases, too much. To gain control of the
amount of air being forced through the tuyere you
will need to add an air intake valve to your air
source. The valve controls the amount of air that
your source can take in and so limits its output.
Usually a piece of sheet metal that covers the intake and pivots on a screw will suffice.

FIRE MANAGEMENT

Fire management begins with the coal. Blacksmith's coal is a clean grade of bituminous coal
that comes either powdered or in pea-sized pieces.
If you cannot locate a supplier, look for the cleanest
grade of coal obtainable. The cleanest coal will
have a sulfur content below 3 percent. Ash content
may vary up to about 15 percent, but the sulfur
content should be the deciding factor. Sulfur, when
heated to forge temperatures, will produce gases
that pit steel. Though this pitting may look "au-
thentic" on a piece of ornamental ironwork, it has
no place on tools. At best, it will cause you extra
work during the grinding and refining phase. At its
worst, pitting may ruin a tool. If a high-grade coal
can be found only in large chunks, pulverize it.
(Use a couple of burlap sacks and beat the coal with
a hammer.)

Charcoal was the mainstay of blacksmiths before
the inexpensive transportation of coal. The black-

smith typically made his own. I have forged at charcoal fires—usually when I was out of coal. I have
tried plain, garden-variety charcoal, mesquite, oak,
even coconut charcoal. I have tried stick form,
briquets, and powdered charcoal. Though some of
them produced hot, and apparently clean, fires, all
of them produced such an array of sparks and pop-
ping embers as to render them useless. Perhaps
there was some technique in the making of charcoal by smiths of old that precluded the fireworks.
In any event, I find that modern charcoal is unsatisfactory for forgework.

There are probably as many techniques for "lay-
ing in" a fire as there are blacksmiths. Some are
traditional, some are elaborate—some are both.
Given that the objective is the same—a quick-start-
ing, intense fire that is easily maintained—the
method is not as important as the rituals might
suggest.

I always begin with the ash bin. Use a coat
hanger with a crook at the end to snag the ash out
of the bin. Running it up the tuyere will insure
unobstructed air flow. If there is residue of an earlier fire, sort through the firepot, removing and sav-
ing the *coke* and discarding the *clinkers*. Coke is
easily recognized by its appearance and weight: a
porous lump that is lighter than the rest of the coal.
Usually found around what was the hottest part of
the fire, coke is nothing more than coal that has
been heated to the point where most of the impurities have cooked out, and all that remains is a light,
fluffy carbon. This coke is the heart and substance
of a good fire and is the form of coal that you will
want at the core of your fire. In a properly tended
fire, you will make coke in a continual process at
the edge of the fire.

Discard the clinkers. Clinkers are hard, glassy
masses that usually form at the grate and can
sometimes restrict or divert the airflow through the
grate. They are a by-product of the coking process

and are the melted residue of the coal's ash content. The better the quality of coal, the fewer the impurities, thus the fewer and smaller the clinkers.

Having sorted and saved the coke and discarded the clinkers, you will need to add coal to the forge to bring the level up to 3 inches (80 mm). The uncoked coal should be arranged in a doughnut from the outer edge of the firepot to the edge of the grate, allowing enough room at the center to lay in some kindling. I usually pile the coal a little deeper toward the grate, about 4 to 5 inches (100 to 130 mm).

With the coal laid into this doughnut-cum-volcano shape, take a full sheet of newspaper, wad it, and flatten it out in several layers above the grate. Take an additional half-sheet of paper and twist it into a rope. Lay this rope in a ring at the inner diameter of the doughnut. Place your recovered coke on the newspaper, and sprinkle a few handfuls of powdered coal over the coke. If this is the first fire and you have no coke, use a few extra handfuls of coal dust. Be sure you don't completely cover the newspaper, as it needs air to burn.

Light the paper at several places near the center of the grate. Let it burn until you can see that the fire is well established on the paper and then gently start your blower. Apply the air slowly at first. You will develop a feel for how much air to apply and how soon to apply it.

When the fire first "catches," it will smoke. Depending on how much coal you had to use to start the fire, it may smoke a great deal. The smoke will be thick and yellowish-white (the whiter the smoke, the cleaner the coal) and smell like Pittsburgh forty years ago. As the temperature of the fire rises, the smoke will disappear (the fire becomes hot enough to combust these gases).

Once the fire has caught and has "coked" the inner diameter of the coal, the process of tending the fire begins. Ideally, the rate of coke production at

The forge poker or rake is used to arrange the coal in the firepot.

the inner edge of the doughnut matches or slightly exceeds the rate of consumption at the center of the fire. To effect this balance, the smith must constantly tend the fire. The newly made coke must be drawn into the center of the fire, and the next layer of coal must be brought closer to the fire so that it, too, will coke. At the same time that this coal-to-coke cycle is being maintained, the fire itself must be contained to keep it from spreading through the firepot. You want only enough fire to heat the material that you are forging.

To cycle the coal to coke to fire, I use a small, pokerlike tool that I made at the forge. I have seen elaborate renditions of this tool that have wooden handles and scroll work, but a simple ½-inch (13-mm) rod, flattened and bent into a handle at one end, and flattened and crooked into a small rake at the other end, does the job. The small rake, ¾- to 1-inch (19- to 25-mm) wide and about 2 inches (50 mm) long, is large enough to move the coke and coal efficiently and small enough not to get in the way. The flattened and open bend at the handle end allows the handle to cool quickly and to hang at the edge of the forge. It should also be shaped to serve as a comfortable handle.

To limit the size of the fire, most smiths use some form of *sprinkler*. A small tin can fastened to the end of a wooden handle will suffice. Pierce the bottom of the can with four or five nail holes. Filled with water, the sprinkler is then passed over the outer edge of the fire. Using a can without the sprinkler holes will almost invariably result in dousing too much of the fire. Sprinkling is a control measure to keep the whole doughnut from igniting.

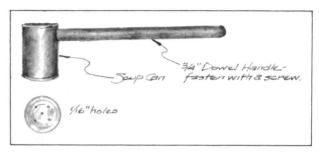

The sprinkler, a fire-management tool, is used to limit the size of the fire. Dousing the coal at the perimeter of the fire keeps the heat under control.

As your forging speed and abilities increase, you may want to add more holes. How close you sprinkle to the heat of the fire is, of course, dependent on how large a fire you will need. Coal at the outer edge of the doughnut ought to be moist but not puddling. It will need sprinkling only occasionally. The water will evaporate more quickly nearer the heat of the fire. You will develop a sense of how often you need to sprinkle next to the coking edge. Look for small patches of smoke rising from the coal, away from the coking edge. These indicate little patches of fire that have found a dry path outside your cycling trace.

To limit fire size and control the fire shape, some smiths use only powdered coal and soak it in water first. They then make a coal-mud doughnut. The advantage to this method is that initially, the fire needs no sprinkling. This sprinkle-free startup lasts perhaps only ten minutes. And though this method produces a tidy, almost sculptured doughnut, I don't think it is worth the time, effort, and mess. I use this method only when working in a strong wind and when the coal is truly powdered. But you should experiment. I know several smiths who swear by this method.

Once the fire is lit and has caught and the inner edge of the doughnut has coked, maintenance of the cycle begins. With the forge rake, draw newly coked coal down into the heart of the fire, and move new coal from the inner perimeter closer to the fire. The importance of maintaining this cycle can't be overemphasized. At the heart of the fire coke, and only coke, should be burning. The raw coal, with its sulfur and other impurities, would pit your forging.

Before attempting to forge a tool, practice the cycle on a piece of scrap steel. Get a feel for how the fire looks when it is burning clean and for the rhythm of stoking the fire. It will not require hours of practice. The whole process will quickly become automatic. It is a little like riding a bicycle: If they had to consider each of the motor skills required, cyclists would have to be geniuses.

The intensity of the fire is judged by the color of its light. The nearer to white the center of the fire is, the higher the temperature. More coke and a stronger draft from the blower will elevate the temperature. For your purposes, a yellow heat verging on orange is all that you will need. I prefer this color of heat — about 1,700°F (952°C) — because I depend on the steel almost blending into the color of the fire before I begin forging. When the steel begins to appear shadowy in the fire, it has "reached temperature." That means that the steel is about 1,500° to 1,600°F (840°C to 896°C) and ready to forge. A hotter fire makes it more difficult to determine the steel's temperature. A white-hot fire — which may well be over 2,000°F (1,120°C) — could easily burn the steel when the steel becomes shadowy in appearance. Also, a truly intense fire may not heat the steel thoroughly. I prefer to be certain that the steel has been "soaked" with heat. The chances of striking a piece of steel whose core has not reached forging temperature, and possibly cracking the steel, are reduced. As in so many other things, taking the time required to do something with assurance is much more efficient than haste and chance.

Even though you carefully soak your steel in the

fire and carefully maintain the proper color of heat, you may still err. You may crack a forging. If a crack is superficial, you need to evaluate honestly how it may affect the end product. If the crack is serious, you need to give it up. Although you can sort of "forge over" the crack, that is, fold it into the core and make it less than obvious, it will always be there structurally.

You may overheat a piece of steel. It is usually the thinner sections that burn—the thinner sections that become the cutting edges. It may not burn and sparkle with a white shower of sparks. It may just have been left in long enough to turn to a white incandescence. Again, you need to evaluate the damage. Harden the steel. Test it with a file. If it will not harden, it will not make a cutting edge. How large is the affected area? Can it be ground away and still produce the tool? If you grind away the damage, be sure you grind until the steel sparks clean and brightly as it should. Ignoring or hoping that all the burnt steel has been removed can be very disappointing. It is much easier to test the material at the time of the error than to compound the error by continuing with some vague hope that there was no error, or that some sort of luck is involved. If there is any such thing as luck, it is in maintaining control and direction continually and discovering at the end of the process that the result was better than you had expected. There really is no other luck in metallurgy.

THE ANVIL

If the forge is the heart of the shop, the anvil must be its soul. While the forge softens the hard, rigid steel into a soft, semiplastic state, the anvil serves as the mold, platform, and third hand to the smith in making the steel behave as it should. It molds the form and develops the potential of the steel. We play the steel against the shapes of the anvil. We can flatten the steel, lengthen it, widen

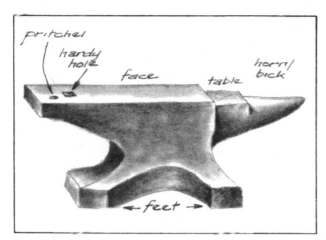

Generally, the larger and heavier the anvil, the better.

it, even thicken it. We can punch holes in the steel, cut it, and twist it. We can mold the steel, rounding it, squaring it, or creating any variation in between. And we can do all of it against the functional anatomy of the anvil.

Of all the smith's tools, the most universally recognized is the anvil. From cartoon animators to poets, the anvil has served as a source and symbol of weight, utility, and steadfastness. Having evolved as a matter of utility, the anvil exists today in nearly the same shape as it existed a thousand years ago . . . a sculptural synthesis of form, function, and technological evolution.

There are literally hundreds of different types of anvils: from huge 500-pound models that must have been a delight to use for their stability to the small and delicate jeweler's anvil that gleams with its polished surfaces. For your purposes, an anvil of 100 or more pounds (45 kg) is ideal. If you don't have a place to install the anvil permanently, it must be light enough to move without too much difficulty. Mine is a mid-nineteenth-century anvil that weighs about 150 pounds (68 kg). That's as much as I can safely manage to move . . . particularly after a day of forging.

There are two courses of action in purchasing an anvil: new and used. If you look at new anvils, the expense is significant. Expect to pay three or four dollars per pound. Be cautious of the "bargain" tools that you will find. A number of Third World countries are producing tools that have the appearance of quality tools but do not perform well. Some are apparently inexpensive castings that are too soft to hold their shape or ring so badly as to render them useless, even for limited work. Physically check the anvil that you are going to buy. Test it with a hammer. It should spring back. The face should be a carbon steel and not a plain casting. Plain cast iron will produce a thunklike return. Listen to the ring. Many of the castings are hollow. The hollow ones will ring more like a bell and less like an anvil.

Used anvils were plentiful at one time. Every farm in America had an anvil. The steel drives of World War II did much to deplete the stock. Antique dealers continue to deplete the stock (as well as drive the prices upward). Of those anvils that come up for sale today, many are in poor condition. Many have been abused or neglected. My own anvil is not a pristine tool. Often the edge on one side of a used one has been chipped in several places and the face no longer smooth. Luckily, I was new to smithing when I bought mine, so I merely turned the anvil around and forged from the opposite side. (For right-handed smiths the horn should point to the right. Forging with the horn pointing to the left has not been a problem for me.) I could probably repair my anvil—hardface it and surface grind it or even weld a tool steel plate on the face. There is enough material left that I could smooth the chipping block and the horn, and square the shoulders on the pritchel and hardy holes. But it would not be the same anvil. It is a tool that, despite its irregularities, I have become more than familiar with, or accustomed to. It is a tool that I am now comfortable with and perhaps even dependent upon. I know its topography as well as I know my own hand. I know where to strike with the hammer to maximize the force and where to lay a piece of steel to straighten it. More than any other tool used by the smith, the anvil becomes his constant. Grades of coal and steel will vary. Hammers wear out, are reground and modified. Tongs are changed to suit the job. The anvil, however, remains that one unchanging and unchanged truth . . . its own reality. When you buy one, consider that it will become the soul of the shop.

An alternative to buying an anvil, at least initially, is to make one. Railroad rails make light but excellent anvils. The rail ought to be used rail, as the train traffic will have work-hardened its surface. Heavy machinery castings can be made usable as well. If the casting itself is not durable enough, a steel plate can be welded to its surface. With a little scavenging and a little ingenuity, an anvil can be made.

Regardless of the type of anvil you obtain, it will still need a stand. Traditionally the stand was a tree stump. It provided additional weight to the anvil when the anvil was secured to it, and it absorbed some of the vibrations and sound as well. Sinking the stump a foot or so into the ground will provide a good anchor. If the stump is freshly cut or will be in the direct sunlight, it should be bound with wire or strapping to limit the amount of checking that will occur in the wood.

Securing the anvil to the stump, especially if it has to be removed for storage, can be a little tricky. Before I permanently mounted mine, I used hanger screws turned into the stump and metal straps with holes in the ends (plumber's tape) that fit over the bolt end of the hanger screws. The straps were then tightened on the hanger screws with nuts. The more securely the anvil is attached to the stump, the more the weight of the stump contributes to the solidness of the anvil.

The height of the anvil is determined by the

The correct working height for an anvil is the height
at which your knuckles just brush the anvil's face.

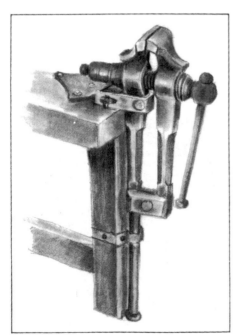

The leg vise provides not only a great grip, but with
its mass secured, it becomes a substantial third
hand as well.

height of the smith. Ideally, the height should
maximize the energy delivered by the hammer to
the object being forged. To determine this height,
stand next to your anvil. Extend your hammer arm
downward. Curl your fingers so that when they are
bent at the second joint they just touch the anvil's
face. This height will maximize the travel of the
hammer, while still keeping the face of the hammer parallel to the anvil's face.

THE VISE

For bending heavy stock, folding metal, hacksawing, cold chiseling, filing, or any number of
tasks common to toolsmithing and metalwork, a
tight-jawed, heavy vise is a necessity. A good vise
should hold the material securely and absorb the
torque, shock, and shatter of your work.

I like having two vises: a leg vise and a machinist's vise. I use the leg vise for forgework. It is heavy
and mounted on a framework that ties directly to
the shop's structure; it is rigid. The long handle of
the vise allows for a great deal of "squeeze" at the
jaws. The leg vise has been, and continues to be, a
basic blacksmith's tool. Unfortunately, I know of
no current manufacturer. Worse still: leg vises are
gaining value on the antique market.

The machinist's vise is a much more common
tool. In fact, most of the world's emerging econo-
mies seem to have invested in foundries that are
producing these vises at a tremendous rate. The
quantities produced and the cost of the labor involved have also made them inexpensive. And
though the work is frequently not first-rate, the
vises themselves seem solid enough. Before you
purchase one, however, back the jaws all the way
open and then all the way closed to insure that the
screw does not bind.

The machinist's vise is, to me, a little like a
woodworker's bench—nothing abusive is done
directly on or into the vise itself. I do not drill into
the vise or use it as an anvil. Tightening the jaws

is done only by hand. Once you use a hammer to tighten a vise, you will need a hammer to tighten it forever after. I like my vise clean—jaws, screw, box, and all. The jaws are flat, parallel, and tight so that they hold the work without crushing or marring it. For holding soft metals or steel that is polished, I use a set of soft jaws. These soft jaws are nothing more than copper or aluminum strips that are folded to hang down from the top of the jaws and cover their clamping faces.

Securely mounted to a bench or stand, the machinist's vise is the perfect platform for filing. With the lines of the vise clean and unblemished, the filework seems easier to reference during the stroke.

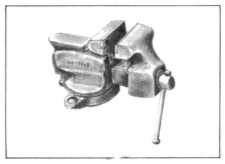

A well-maintained machinist's vise, with its jaws parallel and tight, is an excellent platform on which to do careful, controlled work.

HAMMERS

It is the hammer that brings ring and rhythm to the anvil. It is the direct energy of repeated hammerblows that molds and shapes the steel against the rigidity of the anvil. The shape of the hammerhead and how it makes contact with the steel determines how the steel will be moved. Even though a well-equipped blacksmith's shop may have more than a hundred hammers, three will get you through the projects in this book.

2½ lb. cross peen hammer. The cross peen hammer is among the smith's most versatile hammers. The axis of the cross peen, in relation to the axis of the forging, determines how the steel will be moved. If the peen strikes perpendicular to the long axis of a bar, the bar will be elongated or, as the smiths say, "drawn out." It will lengthen and become thinner without becoming much wider. If you rotate the orientation 90 degrees, the bar can be made wider without becoming much longer. After cross peening, use the flat face of the hammer to flatten and smooth the peen marks.

12 to 16 oz. ball peen hammer. The ball peen of this hammer, like the cross peen of the previous hammer, is used to move metal. The ball, however,

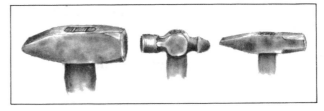

A basic set of hammers. Left to right: 2¹/₂ lb. cross peen, 12 to 16 oz. ball peen, 8 to 12 oz. tinner's hammer.

moves the metal equally in all directions. It is used to spread out the steel. Like the cross peen hammer, the flat face of the ball peen hammer is used to flatten and smooth the peen marks. Select a smaller size ball peen hammer so that it may double as a finishing hammer. After most of the forging of a tool blank is complete, it will have large flat areas, like facets, and some hammermarks will still remain. Rather than trying to lighten the blow of a heavier hammer, use a light hammer to finish the surface. This process is termed *planishing.* Strictly speaking, a planishing hammer has a perfectly smooth, flat face and is used gently to flatten, or at least reduce and refine the shape of previous hammermarks. The idea is to minimize the amount of grinding that must be done later. Planishing hammers are expensive and hard to find. It is much easier to grind the face of a standard ball peen hammer flat. Keep the face as flat and smooth as possible. Whatever deformities there are will be transferred directly to the forging. A smooth, flat planishing hammer will produce smooth, flat planishing marks. The smoother and more refined the forging, the less work that will have to be done at the grinder.

8 to 12 oz. tinner's hammer. Basically a scaled-down version of the cross peen hammer, the tinner's hammer is very useful for delicate forming or where the forgings are small. It is also useful for its intended purpose: cold forging the heads of rivets.

Maintaining a hammer is not usually a topic of

heated discussion. In fact it's seldom mentioned
. . . even in polite company. Next to the knife, it is
probably the most used tool on the planet; almost
every trade uses some form of hammer. Yet almost
no one mentions maintenance. How much maintenance can there be to a tool with no moving parts?

Look at the handle first. Hickory. It is a wood
that is about 20 percent stronger than oak and has a
natural spring to it. If the handle is loose in the eye
of the hammerhead, rehandle the tool. A loose
hammerhead is not only dangerous, but it also does
a poor job of hammering. The looseness of the head
lessens the energy of each blow. Quick fixes, such
as glycerine solutions or soaking in water, are tem-
porary at best. The wood fibers swell with the
moisture. Usually, they swell beyond the capacity
of the hammer eye. The result is that the wood
fibers break. When the wood returns to its usual
moisture content, it is looser than it was before the
soaking. Changing the handle is the only sure way
of repairing the hammer. Maintaining the handle is
a matter of keeping it out of harm's way. Store hammers out of direct sunlight; the ultraviolet rays of
the sun break down the cellulose. Keep the hammer out of moisture. No matter what the age or the
finish of the handle, the wood will expand when
left in contact with moisture.

The hammer's head requires maintenance as
well. As a plain carbon steel, the head is, of course,
subject to rust. If the rust continues for a period of
time, it may pit the hammer. In addition to pitting,
hammer faces are often scarred. There are a hundred different causes for scarring, including long,
hard, honest work. Hammer faces are obviously
not sacred . . . not when we consider what some
hammers are used for. If the face is scarred, regrind
and polish it. Used hammers will invariably need
to be reground (no one seems to dispose of a perfectly good hammer). At the same time, do not neglect the hammers that are already in your shop.

A properly dressed hammer has a slightly domed face.

Dressing a hammer face is really no different from sharpening a knife. The difference seems to be that almost no one will tolerate a dull knife, yet almost everyone will tolerate a scarred hammer face.

When dressing a hammer face, remember that it should be slightly domed. The dome is there to make the most out of every hammerblow. If the hammer face were absolutely flat, each blow would have to be perfectly in line and parallel to the object being struck. The human body, however, works in arcs. Arcs are difficult to align and predict. And with all the three-dimensional possibilities of the hammer face, the anvil, and the object being forged, it would not be possible to shape anything. The dome, then, is a compromise, but a necessary one.

Using a hammer effectively with an anvil requires a little practice. The stereotypical caricature of a blacksmith is an enormous creature with a huge chest and bulging biceps, which dwarf his already diminutive head. And while some may feel this way after that first full day of forging, it is not a requirement. Using a hammer properly requires more coordination than brute strength. By capitalizing on the natural bounce of the hammer off the anvil, the force to raise the hammer is greatly reduced. The "fall" of the hammer ought to be, as the word implies, as much a result of gravity as manpower. The wrist, the elbow, and the muscles that move them are used as much for steering as they are for moving. No one can stand at the anvil and hammer, hour after hour, relying only on the strength of his arms. Learning to control and exploit the hammer, rather than developing the musculature to drive it, is the secret of good hammerwork. Once you discover how this work is done, you'll also discover a rhythm to the work. The rhythm, once you have it, will allow you to sustain the hammerwork while concentrating on the object being forged.

Beyond this governing rhythm of hammerwork, all else is secondary. Almost every smith has his or her own variation on the stance. The feet are usually staggered shoulder-width apart. Some smiths hammer with the hammer-side foot forward. Others are the reverse. Most stand very close to the anvil and try to get their upper bodies directly over the anvil's face. And though it may sound too obvious to mention, keep your head to the side of the hammer's arc.

To get a feel for the bounce of the hammer, stand at the anvil and bounce the hammer off the face of the anvil. Bounce the hammer repeatedly, experimenting with how slow or how fast the blow must be for you to effectively control its impact. Lengthen and shorten the arc. Try hitting other

Hammerwork is first and foremost a coordinated activity of rhythm and accuracy. It is also a balance of the hammer's energy and the smith's control.

Tongs are available in a variety of sizes and jaw styles.

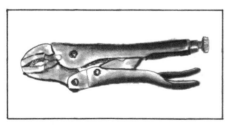

Visegrips are handy to use, particularly for small work.

spots on the anvil. The bounce is different. Toward the center of the anvil the bounce is snappier. What sort of sound is produced where on the anvil? Different hammers respond differently. Large, heavy hammers will work at a slower cadence. Small hammers will have a more rapid beat. It will all quickly become second nature. Soon you will know where and how to "strike while the iron is hot."

TONGS AND THE LIKE

Tongs are the traditional tool for smithing. The varieties available, both new and used, are extensive. The only major drawback to tongs is that to fit each job properly, one would need an enormous array of tools. I buy used tongs regularly. When I find them at the right price, I buy them even though I have an identical set. I will save and modify these tongs at the forge to fit a particular job. Because tongs are mild steel, they forge easily. For work that will not fit the tongs that I have, particularly small forgings, I use Visegrip locking pliers.

Visegrips, which, incidentally, were invented by a blacksmith, seem to be the nearest thing to a universal holding device available. Though they come in myriad shapes now, I still prefer the straight, plier-jawed style for most forging. They seem to be the most versatile. Because they do not have as much mass as tongs, the Visegrips tend to get warm quickly. Cooling them in the water barrel not only makes them more comfortable to hold, but it also keeps the heat from annealing the locking spring. A squirt or two of lubricant after forging prevents rust from making any headway inside the pliers.

QUENCH BATHS

As a matter of both safety and good shop management, it is a good idea to have 15 to 20 gallons (55 to 75 liters) of water handy. I use a small, lidded garbage can that is light enough—even when filled—that I can pick it up and direct the water as a fire extinguisher, if necessary. This amount of water is also sufficient to provide water for the sprinkling can and for quenching at the forge. It *must* be a metal container. Plastic containers are easily ruptured by red-hot steel.

A 15- to 20-gallon (55- to 75-liter) container will suffice for all of the projects in this book — even for multiples of the projects. If, however, during the course of time and experience, you begin to do a lot of heat-treating, 15 to 20 gallons (55 to 75 liters) may not be enough volume to handle the increased heat. Larger forgings may overheat the water. Remember, the water quench ought to be somewhere between 70° to 90°F (21° to 32°C). If the quench gets warm too quickly, you may need to move to a larger container. Maintain the smaller container, but have available a 30- to 50-gallon (110- to 190-liter) container as well. I use a 33-gallon (125-liter) wine barrel for heavy work, but I keep the smaller can handy. (It still functions as a fire extinguisher.)

I like having lids for the containers. Lids will reduce the amount of scum that seems to always collect in open containers. This is not some personal fetish of hygiene, however. During the quench, a tool in red-hot condition is very chemically reactive to anything that touches its surface. Scum on the surface of a quench bath could easily adhere and be burned into the surface of the tool during a quench. Such a "scum burn" could scar the tool.

Not all tools require a water quench. Thinner-sectioned tools and some of the special alloy steels require an oil quench. Choice of oils varies from smith to smith. Some use motor oil (it should be a clean, new motor oil). Others prefer any number of commercially prepared substances. Some old-timers prefer lamb renderings. I have come to prefer olive oil. First of all, it does the job of quenching. Though I have no way of determining the depth of case when hardening with olive oil, the results indicate that it is adequate. Second, olive oil is less messy than a petroleum product. An accidental drip, or even a splash, is not a major concern. Motor oil tends to remain on the floor after cleanup and sticks to the soles of your shoes. The olive oil seems to evaporate, or at least become absorbed without a surface residue. Third, olive oil is more flash-resistant than petroleum. And while a bath fire is always a concern with any oil used as a quench, olive oil seems much less likely to ignite. During the two years that I have been using olive oil, I have not had a single flash. The final point in favor of olive oil is its smell. Motor oil smells like motor oil, only more so when it is vaporized during a quench. Olive oil smells more like a kitchen . . . fresh, natural, pleasant.

The choice of container requires additional thought and energy. Because an oil fire can be a somewhat regular occurrence (expect and anticipate a fire each time you quench in oil), the oil container has to be a fire-control device. I use an industrial oily rag container that has an airtight, foot-operated lid. When the oil flashes (*flash* is perhaps an overstatement—the flash occurs when the escaping gas from the superheated oil is ignited and burns on the surface of the oil), all I do is release the tool into the bath; the lid snaps shut and smothers the fire. It all takes no more than a moment and the fire is out. Do not use water on an oil fire. In addition to making a mess out of the oil bath, it will not extinguish the fire. Smother an oil fire.

Cans with separate lids should not be used to hold oil quenches. It requires too much thinking on the part of the operator, who will, at the time, be too distracted to think logically.

GRINDING AND POLISHING EQUIPMENT
THE GRINDER: ROUGHING AND SHAPING

Many woodworkers cringe at the mention of a grinder. It has a reputation for breathing fire and eating tools. Grinders are noisy machines that throw sparks and sound as though they are one rpm below self-destruction. A grinder seems to be that one item of equipment, whether bought or inherited, that sits in a corner of the shop, gathering dust, biding its time until, like some Aztec god, it will demand and eventually receive a sacrifice. It's an ancient ritual. You offer up a precious chisel and Quetzalcoatl consumes it.

Usually the grinder is used as a last resort. A tool edge has a nick that would take you an hour to remove on the benchstone. You walk to the grinder apprehensively, but with the hope that Quetzalcoatl is still satisfied from your last offering. You think, "Maybe I'll grind just a little bit, then get back to the benchstone." Your whole strategy is to do as little "damage" as possible. So conditioned, you believe in the grinder's innate evil and rapacity—and you are seldom disappointed.

The grinder's infamy is due primarily to lack of information and training. Typically, a woodworking course that deals with the maintenance and operation of equipment focuses more heavily on expensive power equipment. When a student is confronted with a dull chisel, he or she is told: "The grinder is in the corner. The stones are in the tool room. But be careful. You can ruin a chisel." So much for instruction. The same instructor (who is probably doing no more than repeating the warnings that he received as a student) would not dream of sending a student to large shaper with no more instruction than "The on-off switch is on the side. The cutters are in the cabinet. But be careful. That thing eats wood."

The grinder is really no different than many pieces of woodworking machinery. The same operation could be done manually, but the addition of power allows it to happen much more rapidly. The major difference is in the material being worked. A piece of wood that is burned on a sander can usually be salvaged. By removing the superficial discoloration, we've removed the error. When you "burn" a tool edge, that startling rainbow-blue discoloration is not the problem; it is only an indication of the problem. The real problem is inside the steel—it has been changed, softened, and will no longer hold an edge.

Though there are remedies for a burned edge, the obvious solution is to avoid burning. You could remove the power from the grinder, but hand grinding is slow, awkward, and best accomplished by three-handed woodworkers. There is a time and place for hand grinders. I own and use one. I just don't feel that the time and place is when the power is on in the shop.

Grinding requires calm and patience. The calm comes as a steady, even breathing, an unflinching eye. It is ultimately a quiet confidence that grinding is a positive, useful process. The patience has to be twofold. First of all, grinding, like most skills requiring hand-eye coordination, takes practice. Second, grinding is not as fast a process as it might sound. Despite the rumblewhir of the wheel, the sparks, and the vibrations, safe and accurate grinding takes time. Be patient. Remember, no matter how slowly the grinding goes, it is still faster, much faster than a benchstone.

The machine. There are five parts to the grinder. The base of the grinder is probably the least crucial part. Its primary function is to provide secure attachment to a bench or stand. Usually, the base has slots built into the feet for bolts. Use lock washers with the bolts; the amount of vibration set up by the grinder will loosen the nuts if you don't. The second function of the base is to distance the grinder from its stand. This distance is easily adjusted by building up the base with blocks during mounting. If you find a grinder that is otherwise suitable, the base height can be altered.

The second part of the grinder, and one that is

The grinder is a tool basic to toolmaking, used for shaping and sharpening.

not so easily modified, is the motor housing. The distance between the wheel and the motor housing, as seen in the illustration, is a critical factor. Too short a distance can limit your maneuverability; tools "dead end" into the housing before you can make a complete pass. Better-quality grinders avoid this limitation by reducing the diameter of the motor such that it is an inch or two less than the diameter of the stones and by extending the length of the shafts. Better-quality grinders are also five to ten times as expensive. Within the motor housing are the bearings that support the shaft. They should be ball bearings. Although even today's less-expensive import models have ball bearings, there are a number of early models that have bushings instead of bearings. These grinders ought to be avoided. With any sort of heavy use, these "bearings" open up. At that point, the stones will no longer spin true, and vibration can become too exciting for the concentrated work that you will be doing.

The third part of the grinder is the motor. Most motors turn at 3,450 rpm and will vary in horsepower from ⅓ to 1 hp. A ⅓-hp motor may tend to bog down under some grinding. As the stone slows down, the heat will not be dissipated as quickly as it should. The object you are grinding will heat more quickly. A grinder with a ½-hp motor is a better investment. It will handle the heaviest grinding you are likely to perform in toolmaking. Larger motors offer greater stability through their increased mass, and they are a delight to use. They are much more expensive initially, however, and replacement wheels or stones are significantly more expensive as well.

The fourth functional part of the grinder is the stones or wheels themselves. Wheel sizes vary (or ought to vary) with the horsepower of the motor; ⅓-hp to ½-hp motors should be equipped with ¾ by 6-inch (19 by 150-mm) wheels. The larger

7-inch (180-mm) and 8-inch (200-mm) diameter wheels are a full 1 inch (25 mm) thick. The two stones that are most frequently mounted on my grinder are a 60-grit aluminum oxide wheel for rough shaping and a 60-grit wheel of friable aluminum oxide that I use for hollowgrinding finished tools. The plain aluminum oxide wheel at 60-grit is probably a compromise. A coarser wheel would speed up the work but would require more finishing afterward. The 60-grit wheel removes metal at about the right speed; not so fast that I grind past the scribe marks, but not so slowly that I lose patience. The friable aluminum oxide wheel is a relative newcomer to the small shop. The friability of the stone means that it crumbles with use. This crumbling action serves two purposes. First of all, the wheel tends not to load. The crumbling action carries away the steel particles that will load a plain wheel. This means that there is a continually fresh surface to abrade the tool. Second, the friable wheel dissipates heat much more quickly than the conventional wheels do. When establishing a cutting edge, a cool wheel is important. At this point you will have established the temper of the tool and you do not want the heat of the wheel to change that temper. Friable wheels are, of course, more expensive — about three times more expensive. Friable wheels also wear more rapidly than conventional wheels, raising the cost of use even more. For this reason, I reserve my friable wheel for hollowgrinding only.

The final part of the grinder is the worktable. Of all the functional parts of the grinder, this is probably the most neglected. Typically, the arrangement is an all-too-small table supported by a flimsy sheet-metal arm and secured by a nut and bolt that constantly loosen. How you deal with the problem is a matter of time and inclination. For some, it will be an engineering challenge to either modify or remake the worktable. Others will learn to live with it. Still others — the salvagers, the scavengers, the honest-to-goodness junk collectors — will know of, or find, a suitable replacement. (My own solution came in the form of an old automobile generator support arm found on a roadside.)

Grinding. Grinding will never become the pastime of the rich and famous. It is dirty, noisy, gritty, and seldom relaxing. But grinding is a part of toolmaking. Think of grinding as a means to an end . . . and be assured that the end justifies the means.

Grinder height is important. The height of its worktable should be slightly below waist level. This allows your arms to be relaxed. Your shoulders should also be relaxed and not hunched. Your legs should be spread a comfortable distance apart and your knees flexed, not locked. When I am grinding, I use my arms and hands as a holding jig, not so much to clamp the tool as to be able to present the tool in the same manner each time to the grinder. For practice, take a piece of steel to the grinder and try to establish a hollowgrind along an edge. Do whatever you think might work so that as you move the material back and forth, the wheel continues to cut into the same concave trough. Unless you are exceptionally gifted, what you will see when you examine your practice piece is most probably a series of somewhat parallel marks that intersect and overlap.

Try again, but this time, assume your stance carefully. Pay attention to where your feet are in relation to the grinder and where your arms are in relation to your body. Tuck your elbows into your sides, but do not tighten your muscles. Stay relaxed. Adjust your distance from the grinder with your feet so that the upper torso remains relaxed. You should not be stretching or reaching. Look at how you are holding the practice piece. Will your grip allow you to make a full pass? Be sure your hands are in a position not only to hold the tool comfortably but also to maintain their position without fatigue. The work should be supported by the worktable, but you should still be able to move it freely with your hands. The side-to-side movement necessary for the pass is made by shifting weight from one foot to the other and pivoting at the hips. Do not be embarrassed. The movement will look and feel like the rumba, but look at the results. At worst, the parallel meanderings of multiple hollowgrinds should be close together: an indication of things to come. Some of you will have even produced a single trough that looks machine cut.

If the method does not work perfectly the first time, practice. Once you have the knack, the process will not seem so stilted or awkward. The results will impress you.

There are some general rules to successful grinding. Wheels need to be dressed frequently. Dressing amounts to shaping and cleaning the stone so that its abrasive face is always fresh, sharp, and flat. During use the stone will gradually load up with the material you are grinding. This reduces the number of sharp edges in the abrasive matrix that are available to do the cutting. This loading of steel also increases the grinding temperature. Steel accepts and retains heat much more readily than the aluminum oxide. As the wheel loads with particles, more and more steel is offered in friction against the steel being ground. Because the wheel is not cutting as fast as it should be, you tend to press harder against the wheel, creating more friction. More friction results in more heat. The process rapidly escalates, and if you're grinding to establish a cutting edge, you usually burn the tool's cutting edge.

Dressing a wheel is done with either a star-wheel dresser or a dressing stick. I prefer the star-wheel dresser only because the replacement wheels are easy to find. The dresser is designed to rest solidly on the worktable and to be moved back and forth

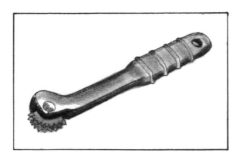

The star-wheel dresser is used to clean and shape the wheels of a grinder. Frequent dressing keeps the wheels clean, promoting quicker and cooler cutting.

with its handle applying both direction and pressure at the same time. The teeth of the dresser tend to dig into the stone (particularly the coarser stones), so a great deal of forward pressure is not required. Start easy into the stone. Only a few passes are required if you dress the wheel regularly.

Another general rule in grinding: Grind only steel. Softer materials will load the stone more quickly than steel. In the case of aluminum, the loading and subsequent rise in temperature may even cause the wheel to explode. Grinders are really single-purpose tools and will only grind *steel* with regular success.

A grinding wheel should be treated much the same as a benchstone. Use the whole surface. Holding a tool in the same place on a wheel does not dissipate the heat effectively, and it will generally scar the wheel, thus requiring additional dressing. It is poor utilization of the tool and accelerates wear.

Then there are the sides of the grinding wheels. Some very competent metalworkers advocate the use of the stone's side. Their reasoning is that it affords a greater surface for use and that the surface is flat. I do not use the sides, and I teach students not to use the sides. There is no good and safe way to dress the stone's sides. As the stone loads, it is rendered useless, or worse, dangerous. Dressing the sides, if it could be done safely, would only diminish the already small grinding edge.

Wear eye protection. Grinders produce small, hot, sharp pieces of debris that will scar the eyes, or worse. An eye injury may end your toolmaking life. Safety glasses ought to be the type that fit snugly against the face and offer protection at the side of the eye as well. Prescription glasses ought to be protected by goggles. Debris and grit will scratch both plastic and glass lenses very quickly.

I wear gloves only when I am rough grinding or shaping a tool. The general problem with gloves is that they build a false sense of security. You tend to push harder and occasionally even press against the wheel. Snug, comfortable, and protected inside your gloves, you tend to ignore warnings such as the steel turning red or your fingers getting too close to the wheel. You lose some of your sensitivity with gloves. I have also seen a few accidents in which the glove was caught between the table and the downward motion of the wheel. In both instances the gloves were sufficiently loose that the operator was able to pull his hand free before any damage was done. Wear gloves, but do not compromise your sensitivity.

When establishing a cutting edge on a tool, I do not wear gloves. I have usually roughed out the cutting edge before hardening and tempering but have left at least $1/16$ inch (2 mm) of material to fine grind. This is the point at which many tools are ruined. Developing a smooth, even hollowgrind across a cutting edge requires patience and sensitivity. Despite the scars and calluses, my hands tell me long before my eyes that a tool is overheating. By not wearing gloves, you tend to take more time at this final grinding. You are better able to sense attitude and movement as you maintain a constant approach to the wheel.

A final note on grinders. Buy new stones. A scrounger by nature and an improviser by necessity, even I buy new stones. A new stone carries with it some assurance that it has not been mistreated or mishandled before it reaches your shop. There is no assurance with a used stone. It may have been dropped. It may have an internal fracture. It may disintegrate under a load. The disintegration will occur when that outer edge is moving at more than 60 mph (100 kph). Disintegration does not really describe the event; it can be much more.

SANDERS: TRUEING AND SMOOTHING

A floor-model disc sander can be a very useful metalworking tool. Unlike the grinder, the disc is meant to be used across its broad face and it presents a broad flat face as the working surface. For smoothing outside radii and flattening relatively broad surfaces, the disc sander is an excellent tool. It is not a grinding tool, however. For the amount of metal that can be removed per disc, the grinder is a much more economical tool. The disc sander is really a light shaping or surfacing tool. Major stock removal ought to be done at the forge or at the grinder first.

The disc sander can also be used as a marking tool. When trying to flatten faces or straighten edges at the grinder, it is handy to be able to use the disc sander to identify and isolate the high and low spots on the surface being worked. The disc leaves a much different pattern on the surface than does the grinder; it highlights the topography.

The belt or disc sander, although primarily a wood-working tool, is also an excellent metalworking tool when used with care.

While special metal-cutting discs can be bought for the disc sander, I use standard woodworking discs of aluminum oxide. Though these discs wear more readily than the metal cutters, I find it too bothersome to switch discs. (The metal-cutting discs do not work well on wood.)

The most important consideration in using the disc sander for both wood and metal (as it will be for any woodworking tool) is sawdust. Before you start sanding metal, be certain that the tool is free of dust. Sawdust can burn very slowly, smoldering with little visible sign of fire. The smoldering, depending on the conditions, can last for days before the fire bursts into flame. After using the sander for metal, it is a good idea to dust the machine before using it on wood. The bits of metal and grit will embed themselves in the much softer wood.

Another safety consideration with disc sanders is the placement of the worktable in relation to the face of the disc. The distance between the edge of the table and the face of the disc ought to be as small as possible. The nearer the table is to the disc, the better the work is supported. Avoid allowing any work to drop below the level of the table into that thin space separating the table and the face of the disc. As often as not, the object will wedge itself in the space. If the motor is very powerful, the disc plate may end up distorted. A weaker motor may only stall and burn out. Depending on how you hold the object, your hands may be in jeopardy. Avoid that crack.

A floor-model belt sander will serve all the same purposes the disc sander does and has the added advantages of (1) generally offering a larger flat surface than the disc; (2) producing striations that are straight (as opposed to the concentric swirls left by the disc); and (3) running cooler than a disc because of the belt's larger size. As with the disc sander, the belt sander is more of a finishing tool. Belts will wear too quickly if used for heavy work. The one additional safety consideration for the belt sander is the seam in its belt. Just as one is careful in sanding wood to avoid digging into the belt, care needs to be taken in sanding steel. The steel is both harder and sharper than the wood, and may do damage to the operator if caught by the belt. Tools should be presented to the belt so that they offer no snag, or way of biting into the belt. If this streamlining is not possible, consider alternatives. There are almost always alternatives in the shop.

POLISHING HEADS AND WORK ARBORS:
FINISHING AND POLISHING

Rough shaping is done at the forge and grinder. Trueing and smoothing are done with sanders. To finish and polish a tool requires finer abrasives. Most discs and belts stop at about 150- to 180-grit. A mirror finish will require sanding down to 600-grit and polishing afterward.

The faces, including the cutting edges, of commercially manufactured tools are considered finished at 120- to 150-grit. This is normally where you come in as a woodworker. When you purchase a tool—a chisel perhaps—you expect that it will take you an hour or two to remove the coarse mill marks from its back. You allow this time because, though the tool was milled by a machine, it may or may not be flat. After a few trial passes on a benchstone, you will know the good news or the bad.

In making your own tools, you are already ahead of this point. You know what is and is not flat. If it is a single-edged tool, use a benchstone to smooth the sanding marks on the critical flat side. If you are making a tool as good as any manufacturer makes, then you are ready for heat treatment (either hardening or tempering). If you are after something more, you need to finish the tool. All the faces, edges, and surfaces need to be smoothed and polished. Sometimes it makes more sense to stop at this point. Limited or one-time use tools probably do not merit more work. But those tools you use every day, tools that become an extension of your hands and so reflect your attitude toward your craft, deserve more refinement.

A mirror finish is not equal to refinement. As in finishing a piece of furniture, you try to keep the lines as crisp as possible so that any shaping done is clearly intentional. Sometimes, especially in the beginning, in your zeal to obtain the absolute in smoothness, you round over or "mush out" the definition. It is the same in toolmaking. Tools ought to have a crisp definition.

What is crisp? Crisp is somewhere between sharp and rounded-over. Take the chisel. Once the tang has been forged and ground and the cutting edge established, what do you do with the sides of the chisel? At this point they will be smoothed to 150- to 180-grit. They meet in a perfect edge with both the top and back of the chisel. These edges are "sharp." It would not be pleasant to hold or to use. A small but intentional bevel along each edge at the top would refine this edge but keep it crisp. Where the sides of the chisel meet the back, they need to remain square. A little buffing along this edge will

The polishing head puts the energy of inexpensive electric motors to good use in a metalworking shop.

remove the sharpness without removing the necessary crispness. As you work at your tools, remember that most of them will last your lifetime. Some will even be passed on. The extra time spent at this point is relatively insignificant.

Polishing heads can be used for a wide variety of finishing abrasives. Flap sanders, rubberized abrasive wheels, hard and soft buffing wheels, even small abrasive cut-off wheels can be made useful with a polishing head. I do not recommend mounting grinding wheels. Most polishing heads are neither massive enough nor have bearings good enough for grinding. They are intended for light work: light sanding and polishing.

The speed of the polishing head is determined by the rpm of the motor and the size of the pulley installed. If the motor pulley is smaller than the head's pulley, the shaft speed of the head will be less than that of the motor. If the motor pulley is larger, the shaft speed will be faster. Most polishing heads are designed to turn at 3,450 rpm. If your motor is identified as turning at that speed, your motor pulley should be the same size or smaller than the head pulley. A 1,725-rpm motor could take a pulley that is larger but no more than twice as large. For most attachments, 3,450 rpm will be the indicated safe speed of operation. Accelerating that speed diminishes the attachment's effectiveness. Some attachments, such as the rubberized abrasives, are more effective in the 1,725-rpm range — both in the abrasive's ability to cut and clear, and in your ability to control the action.

A work arbor mounted on an electric motor has nearly infinite possibilities. Motors still turn up at flea markets and garage sales for five and ten dollars apiece. A work arbor can be had for three or four dollars. Put them together and you've created an incredibly powerful tool for less than twenty dollars. Ideally suited to handle attachments such as larger flap sanders, lapidary wheels of different shapes and styles, and the larger rubberized abra-

A work arbor allows buffing and wire wheels to be directly mounted to a motor. Without guards, however, you should exercise extra caution.

sive wheels, the work and arbor can take a heavier load than the polishing head. Nevertheless, it is still not a grinder, and grindstones should be limited to the grinder.

There are cautions you should be aware of when setting up a motor and arbor. First, buy the appropriate arbor. Arbors are available in left- and right-hand models. Determine the motor's direction of spin and buy the matching arbor. With the wrong arbor, the clinch nut will always be loosening during use.

Second, if you do not understand motors or electricity, do not try repairing a motor. Get help. Some acquaintance will have the knowledge necessary to wire a motor that comes without a power cord; or to reverse the direction of spin; or to install a switch. There is no reason to ruin a perfectly good motor by electrically frying it. There is also no reason to ruin a perfectly good toolmaker by reversing his or her direction of spin.

Keep the motor clean during and after use. The motor you picked up at the flea market was probably not intended for the use that you will be putting it to. It may have vent holes for cooling that expose the brushes, field, and armature. Metal debris has a knack for producing its own circuits. Electricity, which is blinder than justice, always seeks the easiest path to ground, regardless of the schematic. If you keep the motor clean, you reduce the possibility of unplanned circuits interrupting your work.

A final note on electric motors, but one that has

broader applications: While it is laudable to be independent and self-sufficient, to do or make things that no one else does, you need to know where to stop. If you suspect that the electrical system that you are drawing from is not sufficient to the task, you need to modify or rewire the system according to the local codes. If your breakers are always tripping, check the breaker and then evaluate the system honestly. If your lights dim when you start a motor, this is also an indication that all is not right. If you do not know enough about electricity to perform an evaluation, get someone whose opinion you trust to do it for you . . . even if you have to pay for it. Both the polishing head and the work-arbored motor require common sense in use. Rotation of the attachments should be toward the user, and the work should be applied to the lower half of the wheel. Most styles of flap sanders are relatively forgiving. Kickbacks are rare. The rubberized abrasive wheels, however, have no tolerance for error. If an object—especially a cutting edge—is presented to the wheel against its rotation, it will dig into the rubber.

Which brings us to the buffing wheel. For some reason, perhaps because the wheels are only cloth or soft felt, you can get a false sense of security at the buffer. Like the other attachments, buffing wheels are to be used below their equators, below that imaginary line drawn through the center of the rotating wheel and running parallel with the ground. Objects presented to the wheel above that equator will be kicked back. Unlike most other attachments, the buffer can also grab hold of an object below its equator, snatch it from your grip, and throw it some distance. The softness of the wheel will catch and hold any irregularity that resists the movement of its surface. The dropped edge of a knife, the corner of a cutting edge, the wing of a gull-winged gouge, all have a potential for problems.

I've watched students for a number of years, and

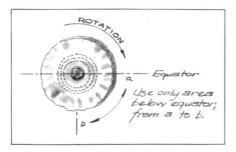

Because they are soft, buffing wheels will grab at edges. Always work below the equator to help avoid injury.

the largest single error I've seen was using too much pressure. Usually, you are a little timid at first. You anticipate the tool being thrown from your hands. When this does not happen, you test the situation. You increase the pressure some and back off. You inspect the piece. Everything is going well. A little more pressure. You inspect again. All seems well. You then begin to reason, "If a little pressure does so well, perhaps a little more would do even better." Your confidence is rising. Pretty soon you are leaning into the work. Pretty soon you are bringing the object up a little to be able to apply more pressure. You notice that the heat is building in the tool, but that it is not too hot. You inspect the tool. It's almost complete. One little corner by the edge needs some work. You return it to the buffer, apply the pressure, turn it a little to be sure that you have that corner and . . . wham! The tool is pulled out of your hands and thrown to the floor (you hope it's the floor, because you *were* working below the equator).

Buffing requires a delicate touch. The buffing compounds can cut only so quickly. Applying undue pressure does not increase their effectiveness. In fact, greater pressure tends to remove the compound from the wheel and deposit it on the object being buffed. (When you see the residue building up on your work, take it as a symptom of too much pressure.) The object being buffed should never get beyond just being warm to the touch (for this reason, I do not wear gloves when I buff). Excessive pressure also distorts the wheel—spreads it out such that not only is there less abrasive to contact the surface being buffed, but the wheel tries to hollow out or flatten it. If this occurs near an edge, the crispness you want to maintain may become "mushed out." A lighter pressure at the wheel means that you can control what you polish as well as its quality.

The second consideration in buffing is the quantity of compound applied to the wheel. You might think that the more compound you use, the faster it will polish. This is not the case. The wheel will only hold so much compound. When you apply the compound (which is called "charging" and is, again, done below the equator), just touching it to the wheel for a few seconds is all that is necessary. The wheel quickly creates enough friction against the compound to melt the binder. As the binder melts, it begins to adhere to the fibers in the wheel, carrying the abrasive with it. If it is to remain on the wheel and do any good, this layer of abrasive needs only to coat the surface. Overcharging just drives the compound into the wheel, stiffening the fibers, which should remain supple. As you use an overcharged wheel, the friction of the work melts the extra compound and the centrifugal force of the wheel ejects it.

Wheel maintenance is the third consideration in buffing. Both overpressuring and overcharging the wheel cause premature wear. Part of maintenance, then (as with most tools), is proper use. Additionally, each buffing wheel ought to be limited to a single compound. That is, for each compound you should use a different wheel. Obviously, a wheel will only polish as finely as the coarsest abrasive that it holds.

Wheel maintenance also requires an occasional raking. As the wheel is used it will glaze over no matter how careful you are. The wheel's surface loses its pliability, and the fibers will not hold a charge properly. Raking removes the glazing and loosens the fibers. Rakes are commercially manufactured for this purpose and are worth the money. An alternative to the rake is a table fork. Like anything else presented to the buffer, it should be used below the equator. With the curve of the tines conforming to the curve of the wheel, gradually apply pressure with the tips, allowing them to dig into the cloth slightly. Repeat this process at different points across the cutting edge of the wheel.

Although the buffing wheel provides the means

for holding and moving the abrasive across the object, it is the abrasive that does the cutting. Buffing compounds come in a great variety of grits, hardnesses, and colors. They also come under a great variety of names that have virtually nothing to do with their function. "Rouge," "Zap!," "Zam," "Kazam," and "Green" offer little indication of which is coarser or harder, or where they would fit in a sequence. A good supplier will know his or her products and be able to recommend a sequence for the carbon steel that you will be polishing.

Not all surfaces require the mirror polish of a buffing wheel. In fact some parts of some tools are more functional if left with the textured surface of the forge. (The shaft of a carving tool, for example, provides a firmer grip if left textured.) And, of course, there is the matter of aesthetics. There is something about the contrast of a smooth, polished head emerging from a dark, textured matrix—something natural yet intended.

Depending on the quality of the coal and the forgework, this dark matrix of the tool is seldom satisfactory as it emerges from the forge. Firescale, that thin, brittle, yet amazingly tenacious skin of oxides, will cover the tool's surface. It must be removed. Removing firescale is most easily done with a wire wheel.

Wire wheels come in a variety of diameters, coarsenesses, widths, and metals. Most cleanup work can be done with a 6-inch (150-mm) steel wheel of medium coarseness. Again, do the work below the equator of the wheel, and use moderate pressure. Heavy pressure, or "horsing" the wheel, does not allow the tips of the wires to cut the scale. It also distorts the wheel, flaring it away from its best cutting path.

ABRASIVES

Modern technology and industry have produced an enormous array of abrasives. The abrasives themselves are harder and sharper than anything that we had hoped for twenty or thirty years ago. And the formats for these abrasives have become incredibly diverse. No longer limited to plain old sandpaper, we have abrasive screen, fiber-impregnated abrasive discs, moldable sanding wheels, sanding string, flap wheels, and, of course, grinding wheels. While we may lament the passing of many things—the five-cent ice cream, a balanced budget, Mickey Mantle—there is nothing that I recall of the "old days" that compares with today's abrasives. They have made toolmaking much less labor-intensive.

Think of abrasives as a system. There are two parts to the system: grit and format. The grit refers to the composition and size of the abrasive. The format is simply how the grit is presented for use, such as paper, belt, flap, stone, and others.

The three most common types of grit are garnet, aluminum oxide, and silicon carbide. I prefer garnet for woodworking, but it is a poor choice for metalwork. Garnet does not wear dull, unlike most abrasives. Instead, it fractures with use, presenting an ever-finer grit to the surface being abraded. In woodworking this is an advantage. The sawdust being produced and the continually fracturing garnet combine to form what amounts to a dry slurry that is very effective at polishing a wooden surface. In metalwork you are after a different result. When grinding or polishing, you strive to produce abrasions that are of equal depth and width. Garnet tends to fracture too quickly against the harder surface of metal, and mushing out is the result. Surfaces tend to be polished in one area and remain more coarsely abraded in others.

Aluminum oxide is harder and much tougher than garnet. And unlike garnet, aluminum oxide fractures very little under use. Aluminum oxide is used extensively in metalwork, and comes in a vast array of formats from plain paper sheets to discs and grinding wheels. Aluminum oxide is the general-purpose workhorse of abrasives.

Silicon carbide, that black to slightly greenish-gray material used on "wet or dry" papers, is the hardest of the commonly used abrasives. Silicon carbide costs about three times as much as aluminum oxide, yet with a little care, it can be made to last five or six times as long. Silicon carbide is also sharper, and so reduces sanding and grinding times. The only real limitation to silicon carbide is the availability of formats. Demand by the public has generally been met by aluminum oxide. To find a broader range of formats for silicon carbide, look in lapidary supply houses and catalogs.

As a general rule, I use aluminum oxide both in grinding wheels and in other formats. I stick with the coarser grits (80 to 180) and use them for general shaping and initial smoothing. Aluminum oxide is relatively inexpensive and comes in larger formats than does silicon carbide. The larger format is handy for removing forge marks while trueing the broad or long surfaces of a tool.

I've been known to use aluminum oxide with a floor-model belt sander to flatten the faces of a chisel. It's much faster and more accurate than trying to file the high points flat and then blending the whole surface with precision. The sander already has the precision built into its machined face. Your focus of effort can then be directed toward holding the tool safely and accurately. Once the preliminary work of removing forge marks and trueing the surfaces is complete, I switch to silicon carbide and use the finer grits (220 to 600) to smooth and polish the tool.

CUTTING EQUIPMENT

THE HACKSAW

Cutting steel is not as difficult as it might seem. In its annealed state, any steel can be cut with a hacksaw or, if it is an intricate shape, a jeweler's saw. But a hacksaw is generally only as good as the money put into it. In most instances, a woodworker's hacksaw is part of a set of tools that was never

intended for serious metalworking. These hacksaws do not hold the blade with sufficient tension
to keep it from twisting. As the blade twists, its cut
wanders from the mark.

In addition to providing sufficient tension, the
saw frame should be comfortable to use with one
hand. Using a second hand on the forward bend of
the frame is too difficult to control. The hands tend
to work against one another. The kerf wanders . . .
frustration. More than adequate cutting pressure
can be applied to the saw with a single-hand grip.
Forcing the cut makes the path more difficult to
control. Again, the kerf wanders; again, frustration. Steady, even pressure on the cutting stroke
(check the arrows on the blade to make certain
they are cutting on the push stroke) and following through with the stroke in a straight line
will produce a clean, well-controlled cut. Short,
fast strokes do not allow proper chip-evacuation
and are, again, difficult to control. The blade
wanders . . .

Every bit as important as the quality of the saw
frame and controlling the stroke of the saw is the
blade itself. Good-quality blades do not usually
come with door-prize hacksaws. Quality blades
will indicate their intended purpose. Steel-cutting
blades are designed to cut steel, and they do a poor
job on nonferrous metals. (Likewise, nonferrous
metal-cutting blades do not work well, or for long,
on steel.) Another thing to look for on the blade
will be the number of teeth per inch (TPI). As in
wood saws, the lower the number, the fewer the
teeth. Hacksaw blades with fewer teeth are intended for cutting thicker material. Finer-toothed
configurations are for thinner material. In order for
the teeth to cut and evacuate chips properly there
should be at least three teeth in contact with the
surface of the material you are cutting. Those
awful experiences that you might have had with a
piece of sheet metal vibrating violently in the vise

while the saw bounced and danced in your hand were probably due to a blade too coarse for the work. If you do not have a blade fine enough for the task, tilt the saw or the work to increase the angle of attack and increase the number of teeth in contact with the work.

Securing the work is the final consideration. Metal—much more so than wood—transfers the shock and vibration of sawing. If the piece will not fit in a vise, clamp it to the bench or to a sawhorse. Secure the piece as close to the cut as possible. The closer the vise jaws are to the cut, the sooner the vise and its mass are able to deaden the vibration. In a long cut, this may mean moving the piece several times. The extra time taken to secure the work is more than made up for by the increase in cutting speed and the quality of the cut.

All the rules for using a hacksaw apply as well to a jeweler's saw. Blades for jeweler's saws, however, are more difficult to find than hacksaw blades. Check with jewelry supply houses, both locally and through mail-order houses.

ABRASIVE CUT-OFF WHEELS

Abrasive cut-off wheels, when mounted on the proper equipment, can be very useful tools. Proper mounting is on a motorized miter box that is intended for this type of work. Miter boxes intended for wood usually do not have sufficient power for the task, and they load quickly with metal dust at the elbow. Miter boxes designed for metalwork also have motor housings that are more protective.

Mounting an abrasive wheel on the table saw is not recommended, and here's why. Using one is essentially a concentrated heating and grinding exercise. The abrasive wheel is fragile to sideloading. If the feeding of the material is anything but steady and directly into the blade, the blade may distort. Abrasive wheels are, by composition, brittle. Distortion on the blade will cause the disc to fail. Blade failure comes in many forms. Sometimes only the rim cracks and ejects the work. Other times the disc simply explodes. Pieces of disc are hurtled from the arbor of the saw at speeds commensurate with the tool's rpm (about 60 to 80 mph). Even a small piece can hurt you.

Despite the disclaimers, I do use an abrasive cut-off wheel. When I happen onto a lucky find of carbon steel stock too long to store, I cut it up using an old wood-cutting miter box. The box stutters, fumes, and occasionally breaks a wheel. Wearing a particle mask, a face shield, glasses, welder's gloves, and a leather apron, I look a little like Darth Vader. But the job gets done and the precautions are worth the extra effort.

I have also used a table saw with an abrasive wheel. It is one reason I recommend against such use.

I like small abrasive wheels. In diameters of 2 to 3 inches (50 to 80 mm), these wheels can be very useful for light, shallow cuts, and for reaching areas just out of reach of the bench grinder. Mounted on a work arbor and with the work supported on a block, the abrasive wheel can be used to make straight, clean cuts of up to 3/16 inch (5 mm). Attempting to cut much deeper increases the chances for side-loading and disc failure.

THE OXYACETYLENE TORCH

For those lucky enough to own an oxyacetylene torch with a cutting head, cutting can be done very quickly. When cutting with an oxyacetylene torch—especially silhouette work—all cuts ought be made at least ¼ inch (6 mm) wide of your mark. The oxygen-enriched acetylene flame actually burns the steel. Depending on your ability to hold parallel to the surface and maintain the speed of the cutting head, you may ruin as much as ¼ inch (6 mm) of material on either side of the cut. If the cut is very long, the amount of grinding required to bring the cut to its mark may negate the amount of time saved by using the torch. For this reason I only use the cutting torch for very rough cutting: reducing a large circular saw blade into storable pieces or cutting leaf springs into lengths of 8 to 10 inches (200 to 250 mm).

Besides speed, the obvious advantages of the torch are not having to secure the stock for cutting, not having to anneal before cutting, and not being limited to a straight-line cut. But the torch has its drawbacks. It is sometimes difficult in the process of cutting to remember what is hot and what is not. If you are cutting on the ground, watch where you put your knees and shoes. Pay attention to where your hoses are. It's not so much that you will cut through them, but if they're on the ground near the cutting area, hot slag or metal can melt them. The final drawback to oxyacetylene cutting is the amount of waste. Remember the ¼ inch (6 mm) of material lost on either side of the cut.

Although the abrasive wheel, the hacksaw, and the torch are all useful tools, the cutting equipment I use most often in toolmaking is the forge and the cut-off hardy cast into the anvil. Heating the steel to a medium cherry color, setting it on the hardy, and striking it with a hammer first on one side, then cutting in on the other, is fast and direct. The uncut portion is easily twisted off with tongs or pliers. The time required is no more than half a minute. More important than the speed of cut is the directness of using the hardy. Make the cut at the tang end. Forge out the head and shaft of the tool and save the extra for the tang. As you draw out the tang, whatever is extra to the tool can be removed from the waste side, and the hardy cut becomes the sharp point of the tang.

ANCILLARY EQUIPMENT
FILES

I have always liked files. Partly because of their usefulness and partly because of their eclectic nomenclature (which appeals to the snob in us all), files have always been intriguing. Besides making it possible to say "flat bastard" in polite company, files are great multipurpose shaping tools. Years ago, in what was then called manual training, using a file properly was nearly a semester course. Given a rough block of steel, students were expected to reduce and shape it to specifications using only files. The amount of work required was not only exhausting but also frequently boring, tedious, and frustrating. It was, however, just enough practice to insure that the technique was learned—for a lifetime.

Most people use a file so seldom that no technique is ever developed. The file rocks back and forth to such uneven pressure that the corners of the work become rounded, and round parts become oblong and irregular.

The first factor for success at filing is the file itself. To be useful it needs to be sharp. To be sharp it needs to be relatively new and unabused. Used files are fine to buy for use as carbon steel stock, but they are regularly disappointing to use as files. Even files that have been lying around the shop (especially in drawers and boxes) tend to lose their sharpness over time. A little oxidization, a little clanking around against other files and the bite is gone. When storing files, wrap them in a cloth after applying a little spray-lubricant. The cloth will serve as a fender, and the lubricant will reduce the opportunity for oxidization.

The cut of the file (the number and arrangement of teeth) needs to match the task at hand. Files come in single-cut and double-cut patterns. Single-cut files are used as smoothing tools and have only

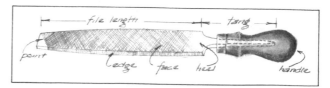

The file, a basic tool of shaping and refining, is easy and safe to use.

one tooth per row. The rows are set at an angle to the long axis of the file. Used properly, a single-cut file will leave a surface ready for 400-grit polishing.

Double-cut files have two rows of teeth that intersect or overlap one another, resulting in a diamond pattern of multiple teeth. The angles of these patterns vary from manufacturer to manufacturer, and according to the tool's function. Double-cut files are for rough work and general shaping. So far, the nomenclature is straightforward: single-cut, double-cut.

Tooth size, or spacing, has its own nomenclature (from coarsest to smoothest): rough, bastard, second cut, smooth, and dead smooth. This nomenclature, however, is used generally only on files of 10 inches (250 mm) or more. Smaller files may have numerical designations beginning with No. 00 (the coarsest) and end at No. 8 (the finest). These designations, both for the larger files and for those under 10 inches (250 mm), are relative to the size of the file. A 14-inch (360-mm) bastard is, therefore, a coarser file than a 10-inch (250-mm) bastard.

The final bit of file nomenclature deals with the shape of the file in cross section. Again, like tooth spacing, the shape of the file is relative to its length: A 10-inch (250-mm) square file has a smaller profile than a 16-inch (400-mm) square file.

Despite the incredible variety of files available, I find myself using only two or three files regularly. For rough shaping I like the heft and cut of a flat bastard 12 to 14 inches (300 to 360 mm) long. I use the same size and cut in a round file and a square file to match other shaping requirements. For finish work, I like a flat second cut in a single-cut pattern, 12 to 14 inches (300 to 360 mm) long.

Using a file effectively requires practice, but not as much as might be expected. As with the hacksaw, many people's experience with the file has been limited to quick fixes: filing a bolt flush with a nut, smoothing the edge of a piece of sheet metal, or perhaps leveling the point of a protruding nail.

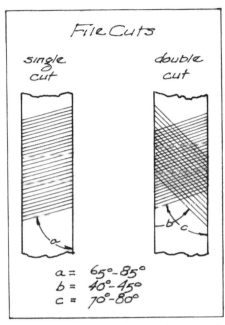

Basic file cut differences. Course angles and tooth angles vary, and should be chosen according to the material to be cut.

We tend to look at files as tools of opportunity—something on hand that will probably do the job.

Files are capable of a great deal more than simple fixes. In fact, all of the tools in this book could be made with just the forge and the file, and in an earlier time they would have been. In the hands of a skilled user, the file can be both an aggressive shaping tool and an instrument of delicate refinement. In its versatility it is like the woodworker's chisel. And like the chisel it requires technique and confidence—both of which require practice.

Filing. Having selected the appropriate file, your next concern is securing the stock. If the stock vibrates or chatters, there is no control to the filing. As in hacksawing, the nearer the stock is to the jaws of the vise, the more effective the vise is in absorbing and deadening the vibration. The work ought to be secured at elbow height or a few inches lower.

Address the stock with your body so that your left foot is pointed toward the stock and almost perpendicular to it. Put your right foot behind the left at a comfortable distance and canted, in a relaxed position, to the right. (Left-handers would of course reverse this position.) Your knees should be flexed, not locked. Bend forward slightly at the waist. This should be a balanced, comfortable position, and one that will allow you to lean forward, flex your knees, and rock on your feet, thereby creating the controlled motion necessary for effective filing.

The next concern is the grip. A proper grip, however, requires a handle. Holding a bare tang with the palm and fingers will not provide the force or control that is necessary. Self-threading, screw-on handles are relatively inexpensive and can be switched from file to file. I personally prefer turning a handle at the lathe and mounting it permanently to each file. (See "Handle-ing a Tanged Tool" in Chapter 4.) Turning or carving your own handles means the handle can be shaped to your hand.

Besides, having the handle permanently mounted tends to cause us to treat the files more as individual tools than as transients. We tend to arrange and store them rather than stashing them in one of those nefarious drawers of miscellany.

Gripping the file is done with both hands. The right hand grips the handle with the thumb on top. Placing the thumb on top of the file handle makes you more conscious of the motion you impart to the file. With that thumb pointed along the long axis of the file, you are better able to sense your control. The left hand grips the other end of the file (more properly known as the point). With the heel of the palm on the point, the fingers curl under the file. This is not a clenched, white-knuckle grip. The left hand is there only to balance the pressure being applied at the handle and so steady the stroke of the file.

About two-thirds to three-quarters of each file stroke should come from the body as a result of the rocking stance. The last one-quarter to one-third of the stroke is done with the arms. The strokes are even and deliberate, unhurried. The push stroke is the cutting stroke, and that's when you should apply pressure. The back stroke, or retrieval, is only a glide. Pressure during the back stroke tends to curl the file teeth forward; if the teeth curl, the file dulls.

The teeth of a file are not all in the same plane. If they were, the file would not cut. As you file unhurriedly with these long, even strokes, you will feel where the file is biting. With a little sensitivity and practice, you will be able to move the bite in a stroke to where you want it. You will be able to anticipate the cut. Surfaces will become flatter, truer. Filing will become less a task and more a means of direct expression.

Drawfiling. Drawfiling is a second method of filing and is used for blending and smoothing an object along a selected axis. Both hands grip with the palms down and the fingers wrapped around the

The cut begins with arm power only. Cut at a comfortable height.

The arms alone power the stroke for about two-thirds of the cut.

With the hands and arms locked in position, the hips and lower body provide the last third of the stroke. When done properly it produces a flat surface.

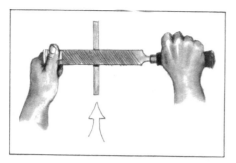

In drawfiling, the file is held perpendicular to the direction of the stroke. A piece of tape at the toe of the file makes the grip easier and safer.

file. Again, it is a firm grip, not a white-knuckled clench. Use your energy for downward pressure and control. Using a single cut file held perpendicular to the direction of stroke, push the file forward to cut. The wide placement of the hands is ideal for maintaining a perpendicular cut. Drawfiling is particularly effective for silhouetting a shape in thin stock.

During use, a file loads with the material being filed. Softer metals such as copper and brass can load a file very quickly. A loaded file cuts irregularly and has a glazed, sliding feel instead of the bite-and-drag feel of a cutting file. To keep your files clean, buy and use a file card regularly. The spring-steel bristles of the card are bent so that they "stutter" and pick at the waste metal lodged in the file's teeth. Three or four strokes are all that is necessary to clean a well-maintained file.

Files are not only useful shaping tools; they can also be used for hardness testing. Files are left in a fully hardened state when manufactured, about 64 to 66 on the Rockwell C Scale. During the hardening phase of toolmaking, you need to verify that your material has been fully hardened. Because you know that the file is fully hardened, testing it against the surface of the tool in question will provide a relative indication. If the file slips across the surface without biting (you may have to clean the firescale from the material to determine for certain), the tool is fully hardened. If the file bites, you will need to reharden your work.

The file you use for testing ought to be sharp. A dull file will not give a true indication. Keep one file pristine, and reserve it for testing only. I prefer a single-cut file because the bite does not score the work as deeply if the tool has been fully hardened.

DRILLS

Boring a hole in a piece of wood is a straightforward proposition. Most of us have bits that were designed specifically for woodworking. Most of these bits take advantage of the relatively soft nature of wood and cut the material quite aggressively. Some cut and dig so aggressively that they can be used safely only in hand-powered tools, such as the auger. This aggressiveness is due in part to the size and angle of the cutting lips and to the flukes, which sever the circumference of the hole before the lips cut it and the flutes remove it. This sever, cut, and remove system works well in wood and is designed as variations on the same theme in the bradpoint bit, the wood auger, and Forstner type bits.

The common twist drill, or metal drill, does not perform as well in wood. The hole tends to mush in at entry and tear out at the exit. Burning, even at reduced speeds and rates of feed, is a common occurrence. These are drills we use in wood when we do not have the appropriate size in a specialty bit. They work. When they are new and sharp (in some shops the only sharp drills are new drills) a metal drill will do an adequate job in a hard hardwood. Usually, though, woodworkers should use a specialty bit whenever they can.

Metal drills are designed primarily for boring holes in metal. But because they are hard and tough and we can apply great pressure to them, they will bore into almost anything. Still, metal drills are most effective for boring holes into metal. It is the

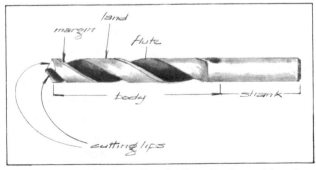

A drill bit and its nomenclature. Note that the cutting lips each have the same angle to the long axis of the bit.

point of the drill that determines how smoothly and effectively a particular drill will bore.

The point of a drill bit is, ideally, the balanced terminus of two skewed scrapers that are shaped to the same angle of attack from the long axis of the bit. The lands of the drill, when properly ground, are the scrapers, and they are called cutting lips. The flutes of the bit—the spiral hollows between the lands—serve to remove the waste during drilling. In a very simple sense, a drill is like two chisels that are wound around a central axis. Because the chisels need a starting point to begin cutting, their edges are skewed away from one another, which makes the chisels push against one another toward their common axis. This self-balancing action helps to keep the bit on line while drilling. The point itself serves to establish the path of the bit.

Drill points vary. Depending on the material being drilled and the type of machine being used, the point of the drill lengthens or shortens. Most commonly, however, the metal drills you have on hand will be *regular point* drills. A regular point drill will have cutting lips ground to an angle of 59 degrees. The lip clearance angle, taken from the cutting edge to the trailing edge of the land, will be 12 degrees. The cutting angle of the lips, which is taken from an end view of the bit, will be 135 degrees. What you need to have clear in your mind is how this affects your drilling.

If there were some way to be inside a bit during drilling, the first and most important relationship you would see is that the cutting lips, if the drill is properly ground, cut at the same rate and at the same time. If the drill were not properly ground and the lips were not equal, you would see the point scribe a small circle and the hole consequently becoming larger than the diameter of the drill. Because there is pressure only against one lip, the bit is forced to the opposite side. The amount of flex in the drill will determine how far the bit distorts. If pushed too far, it breaks. Therefore, the cutting lips have to be cut at the same angle and in the same plane.

Your second observation from inside the drill bit would show that the cutting lips should be the only part of the bit touching the metal. If any part of the trailing edge also touches, it disrupts the balance of the cutting edges and creates additional friction. Again, the bit wanders and the hole is overbored. You may also overheat the bit.

Given these two basic observations, you ought to be able to visualize what is necessary to the shape of a drill point. First of all, the drill point is not a simple cone. Each land is a part of a cone with a different axis. Second, though these cones are on different axes, they are the same cone in size and shape. With these two points in mind, it will be easier to establish and maintain a drill point.

Sharpening drill bits. Drill bit sharpeners and sharpening jigs seem to go through the same flurries of invention, promotion, and marketing that multipurpose kitchen tools do. I admit to not having been immune to these flurries. I own two jigs and one sharpener. They are neatly stored in the back of a cabinet. I keep them as reminders that a good drill bit sharpener costs about $1,000 and not $15, $25, or even $40.

The most effective method of sharpening bits (considering the end result, the amount of money invested, and the amount of setup time involved) is to do it by hand at the benchstone or, if the point is in very poor condition, at the grinder. Now your hands will not consistently produce or reproduce the 59 degrees, 12 degrees, and 135 degrees of a perfect point. But with your hands, and with a clear image of the goal in mind, you will produce a point that will get the job done.

If you take the time to hone a drill at the benchstone each time you use it, you may never have to use the grinder. Sharpening a bit at the stone is like sharpening a gouge. Make contact with the stone at the trailing edge of the land and twist and push the bit, lifting it from the stone just as it comes to the cutting lip. After a few strokes, check the surface to see where the stone is cutting, and adjust your grip and stroke accordingly. This is a system of maintenance and presumes that the bit already has the appropriate angles established. Although this system may seem a bit precious or fragile, it works.

Not all of us take the time required to perform maintenance on a tool before we stow it away. Most of us, in fact, are not that dedicated to organization and efficiency. Most of us will need to use a grinder to sharpen a drill bit. The bit will have been chipped or the cutting lips so rounded that using a benchstone would take hours. Being able to picture the proper relationships in your mind is important as you approach the grinder.

Use a felt tip pen to mark a reference line on the grinder's worktable that is canted at 59 degrees to the grinding edge of the wheel. (The worktable itself ought to be set in such a way that its surface is on a plane that would match the centerline of the wheel.) With the drill held firmly against the table and the drill in line with the reference mark, rotate the drill until the cutting lip is parallel to the wheel, and *do no more than touch* the lip to the turning wheel. Rotate the drill 180 degrees and do the same to the other cutting lip. The wheel marks scored on the cutting lips should be no more than $1/32$ inch (1 mm) wide. If you held the bit in the same position on both cutting lips, and if you held the grinding to no more than a touch to the stone, the cutting lip angle on both lands will be close to 59 degrees. More important than the 59 degrees, the cutting lips will be the same distance and at the same angle to the central axis of the bit.

Having established the cutting lips' angle, you need to next provide for their clearance. To do this you will need to do some sensitive grinding. Rest your left hand on the grinder's worktable holding

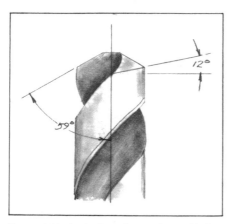

Successful boring is dependent on these critical angles.

the drill's 59-degree angle parallel to the stone's edge. Hold the shank of the drill in your right hand slightly below the left hand (the bit should not rest on the worktable). Rotate the bit so that you can see the cutting lip. Now bring the bit into the grinding wheel with light pressure while at the same time lowering the right hand slightly. Repeat the process three or four times. Grind both lands. Be careful not to alter the cutting lips during this clearance grinding. The clearance angles that you establish may or may not be even on both sides. They will probably be close. As long as it does not weaken the land support for the cutting lip, the drill will bore accurate holes without failure. After grinding, hone the point at the benchstone.

Drilling. Unlike drilling in wood, metalwork generally requires the steadiness of a drill press. It is too difficult to hold a hand drill in a fixed position and apply direct and even pressure. If you let the axis of the drill wander even slightly, you over-bore the hole. There are just too many variables to make hand drilling worthwhile.

The first step in metal drilling is to locate the hole site. Use a metal scribe or a pencil to mark the site, and then centerpunch the exact point. The centerpunch leaves a dimple in the surface that serves as a guide for the point of the bit. Without this little crater, the drill point would wander on an otherwise smooth surface.

The second step in drilling is to properly secure the work independently of your hands. Of all the accidents that I have seen and experienced on drill presses, most were not the result of long loose hair, neckties or loose chuck keys. These accidents were rather the result of the drill bit biting and locking in the workpiece and—because the work was not properly secured—picking it up and spinning it. Unfortunately, when spinning at a few hundred rpm, almost anything is sharp enough to cut.

In addition to using a bit that matches the desired hole size, you may want to drill a pilot hole first. Because my drill press is old and a little loose, I pilot-drill all holes that will be larger than ¼ inch (6 mm). Beyond ¼ inch (6 mm), the cutting lips of the bit are not in the dimple; they are in the web, the solid center axis of the bit. If the drill press is a little loose, the bit will wobble. I keep a ⅛-inch (3-mm) and a ³⁄₁₆-inch (5-mm) bit in pristine condition for pilot drilling. The pilot holes will provide continuous contact for the cutting lips throughout the depth of the hole.

The final concern in drilling is the bit speed. Smaller bits work better with higher rpm and larger bits with lower rpm. Exact rpm requirements can be found on the sides of drill presses, in drill indices, and on giveaway charts. The guiding rule ought to be that the bit turns slowly enough to allow the cutting lips to cut but fast enough to keep the bit from digging. The bit ought to bore evenly and steadily as you apply pressure to the feed handle. Pressure on the handle ought to be light for smaller bits and moderate for larger bits. A two-handed, gut-busting pull will break a small drill and will ruin at least the point on a larger bit. If the bit does not bore with moderate pressure, check its point for sharpness. Also check the material to make sure that it's in an annealed state.

Though it's not a requirement for any of the projects in this book, drilling large or deep holes may require a lubricating and cooling oil. Although there are a number of lubricants available, I generally use olive oil. I have three reasons. First of all, I use olive oil for my quench bath, so it is handy. Second, olive oil cleans up easily. And finally, olive oil works. It is certainly not the toughest of lubricants, but with a sharp bit and the work piece properly secured, olive oil performs very satisfactorily.

THE PROPANE TORCH

The cost of a propane torch is enough to recommend its use. For light silver solder work, tempering, starting the forge in a high wind, mounting handles, even for obtaining critical temperature in small tools, the propane torch is a good investment. Easy to operate and controlled with a single valve, the propane torch is straightforward to use. The most common mistake made with the propane torch is failing to locate the hottest part of the flame.

There are two parts to the propane flame: the large, pale blue brush at the periphery of the flame and the smaller, intense blue cone at the center of the flame. This center cone is hot enough and has sufficient volume to harden small tools. In fact, this makes the propane torch preferable to the forge for hardening delicate forgings.

3

Safety

S afety is all too often something that is set aside and separate from our activities in the shop. We own safety glasses, face shields, dust masks, respirators, ear protectors, and other devices. We are armed for safety. We protect ourselves against accidents. We interpose an instrument of protection between ourselves and harm's way. Safety, as such, becomes an additive, a protective mantle that you come to depend upon. This is unfortunate.

I do not mean to minimize the importance of protective equipment. My own eyes have been saved several times, and probably my lungs, liver, and kidneys are no worse for the work I have done, thanks to protective equipment. But protective equipment is only one part of safety.

Most of you have met people at social gatherings who have, when you were identified as a woodworker, looked at you with an all too familiar look. And you inevitably responded by holding out both hands and saying, "Still got 'em all," while you wiggled your fingers in proof (that is, if you actually do still have them all). A little challenge and a little defiance. People expect you to be missing fingers. Like the scarred cheek of a swordsman or the wooden leg and patch of a pirate, we expect that missing fingers go with the trade. It is, for some reason, believed to be unavoidable and inevitable. We will be maimed.

This is too fatalistic and too morose an attitude to live and work with. Certainly the machinery that you use can be dangerous, even deadly. But the equipment is not inherently dangerous until you turn it on and misuse it. In all the years that I have spent living and working around "dangerous" equipment, I have seen only two accidents that were directly attributable to equipment failure. One was a parachute that failed to open and the other was a grindstone that disintegrated. Every other accident was directly attributable to the operator—the person who made the decision about where, when, and *how* the equipment was to be used.

If you take the perspective that operator error is the root of most accidents, safety must take on a different aspect. If you had no choices about where, when, and how to use your equipment, then protective equipment would be your only salvation. You would be like a bumper car, hurtling and bumping your way through a short, miserable, whiplashed life. Fortunately, you have choices. More important, you have control. Control is there for the taking. The choice is yours.

Taking control is not a verbal or visual process, it is a thought process. Control requires a conscious effort. You need to think through procedures from beginning to end, no matter how often you've done them. It seems easy, but there are pitfalls. They are not insurmountable, but they can be insidiously subtle, like the mesmerizing, steady, almost soothing sound of a table saw that you have used for twenty years — so familiar, so reliable and yet, if misused, so catastrophic.

The first of these pitfalls is boredom. Boredom more regularly attacks those who have lots of experience. You have performed a procedure hundreds, if not thousands, of times. You know how to do it, how to control the machine, how to control the material, how to move your hands, and where to stand. You do your part and the machine does its part. Your eyes are open and you are seeing — but you are not watching. If you are lucky, at some point something startles you and you realize what you are doing. I am embarrassed to admit how many times I have "awakened" to discover that I am on cut number twenty-seven and not number six. How I got this far I do not know, but the subsequent dose of adrenaline is usually enough to keep me on track.

How to avoid boredom? Avoid lengthy repetitions of the same task. Break up the monotony. Do sevcral series of alternating processes. Spell yourself so that you aren't lulled. Most of all, be aware that you are subject to boredom. Know that this boredom is a little like a self-induced hypnosis—the whirr and hum of the machine, the vibration, the repetitive, monotonous movement. Know this beforehand and the knowledge will allow you to focus on the boredom and suppress it.

Another major detractor of concentration is haste. No one is so organized, so methodical, so self-managed, that haste has never touched them. Either self-imposed or actual, deadlines can loom on the horizon like locusts. Deadlines, as they approach, elevate anxiety. Anxiety generally manifests itself as haste. There is sometimes only a thin line between haste and alacrity. Haste is insidious. It begins to creep first into your way of doing things and then, if not checked, into your work. Our evolution is not, I hope, in the direction of least resistance, but rather in the direction of anticipating perfection.

Haste at the work level not only diminishes your possibilities for perfection, but it increases risk. You risk not only the work, but also yourself. No deadline seems worth the cost of a personal injury.

Unfortunately, there is no cure. To recommend that you plan ahead is a little too precious—too thin on reality and too thick on sermon. And, after all, deadlines are what make the world go 'round.

Take a moment to look at what you do in your shop. Fully three-quarters of your enjoyment, enthusiasm, and satisfaction is derived from how you work. Cutting a tight-fitting joint, smoothing a board, delicately shaping a handle are not only a means of communication, they can sometimes *be* the communication. You shortchange yourself and your work if you allow anything to interfere. You risk much more if you allow anxiety and haste to control your work.

The last detractor from your concentration on

working safely is timidity. Timidity is that vague and nebulous feeling that lies somewhere between caution and fear. Caution allows you to proceed. Fear denies you access. Timidity vacillates between the two, and therein lies the problem.

To be used effectively, a tool must be used with confidence. Dangerous tools (and most are dangerous) have to be used with a confidence tempered with caution. If the tool is an old and trusted comrade, your confidence is lightly tempered with caution. You know the tool's limitations. You know your limitations. Caution is the balance. If the tool is new to you, you are looking for the limitations. This is good. Caution is a little stronger than confidence. Caution is there to guide you, to let you discover the limitations.

Timidity appears when you relinquish both confidence and caution and succumb—if only for an instant—to fear. Fear precludes either confidence or caution. More important, fear precludes control. Without the control, you react instead of act.

Timidity is not exclusively the dilemma of the beginner in a particular field. My own personal nemesis is the shaper. Equipped with a large, panel-raising bit turning at 12,000 rpm, the machine howls. And though I have made thousands of passes by the bit, I am never at ease. The sound, the vibration, the mounds of shavings verge on overwhelming. I am cautious . . . very cautious. I know the machine; I even teach other people how to use it. Still, I am cautious. Fences are twice checked. The arbor nut confirmed tight. Elevation locked. A few hand rotations of the spindle. A short burst of power to be certain that everything functions under power. At this point I am better. The timidity is under control. While I am more confident of myself, I am no less respectful of the machine. Satisfied that the machine will do what is expected of it, I can focus on what I expect of myself.

Knowledge, concern, and deliberate action directed toward ensuring safety, all tend to diminish the fear and the timidity and reduce it to a healthy caution. But if the fear remains — and you must be willing to admit fear — *do not use the tool.* There are always other ways.

EQUIPMENT

Your hands and eyes are tools. They relate directly through the material what your mind envisions. The eyes and hands are the most elemental tools of the craftsman. Most of you would not leave a chisel out in the rain. Most of you would not toss a hundred-dollar plane into a corner. Most of you would not willingly neglect a tool. Yet many of you pay much less respect and attention to your most basic, primary, and elemental tools — the hands and eyes.

EYEWEAR

The eyes are incredible tools. Stereoscopic, color-sensitive, rapid-focusing, the eye can pan and zoom at will. Add to that an auto aperture with a self-cleaning lens cover and the human eye would cost a fortune at the local camera shop. And most of you were given two.

Though the eye has remarkable defense mechanisms in the lids, lashes, and tear ducts, it is still a delicate and somewhat fragile instrument. Try to imagine someone taking your favorite camera and placing it next to a grinder. Imagine them removing the lens cap, turning on the grinder, and grinding a piece of steel next to the exposed lens of your camera. Try to imagine it. It's your camera!

The point is obvious. And just as you have a knee-jerk reaction to safeguarding your relatively primitive camera, you should have the same reaction for your much more sophisticated eyes. Camera lenses are replaceable. The eye is not.

In purchasing eye protection I have two criteria: It must meet safety standards and it must be comfortable to wear. Verifying that it meets safety standards is easy enough to do; "Z87.1" etched or raised somewhere on the lens or lens frame indicates that the equipment meets the specifications of the American National Standards Institute. Not all eye protection will have this alpha-numeric designation. Check before you buy.

The second criterion, comfort, is not so straightforward. After years of observing and evaluating my own actions as well as those of others, one all-encompassing, universal truth emerges: safety equipment will only be worn if it is comfortable. Uncomfortable equipment will not be worn no matter what the possible consequences. The rule for any piece of safety equipment is to buy only that which you will wear.

RESPIRATORS

Lungs are a necessary part of the human engine. Unlike the eyes and hands, their impact on our work is not as direct. Ignoring their protection, however, may have a more dramatic effect. While I have met a number of artisans with missing digits, limbs, and eyes, I know of none without lungs.

If you want complete safety, wear a respirator at the forge or the grinder, or anytime you suspect particles or fumes. A step away from a respirator is a particle mask. It will not stop fumes, but it will filter particulates. For those of you who elect to wear no protection, try this experiment. Buy an inexpensive disposable particle mask. Wear it for just one hour at the forge or grinder. Look at it when you are done. A filthy mask communicates much more than numbers and charts representing chemical analyses.

GLOVES

Hands, like the eyes, are incredible mechanisms. Not only do they permit an amazing range of controlled motion and action, the hands also allow you to feel. Even the thickest, work-hardened, weather-beaten, calloused hands have an astounding degree of sensitivity. Much of what you do as woodworkers is only hinted at by the eye but can actually be felt by the hand. How many times have you been stymied by the grain direction in a piece of wood, only to be set right by sensing the surface with your fingertips?

The hands are tougher than the eyes. The cuts, bruises, burns, and skeletal injuries encountered in a lifetime of work, if you viewed them all together, would be inhibiting. Fortunately you have to deal with them only one or two at a time.

In metalwork, the most frequent hazard to the hands is the sharpness of the material. Small cuts from the ever-present edges are about as common to metalworking as slivers are to woodworking. Always assume an edge is sharp. You will seldom be disappointed.

Another hazard to the hands is heat. Although an object may have cooled to dead gray in color, it may still maintain a temperature of almost 800°F (448°C). Taking an extra moment to scrutinize a suspect object with a pair of tongs is a good habit to develop. Sprinkle it with water. If it hisses, you can be happy you are using tongs. If it does not hiss, you have wasted (maybe) twenty seconds.

Gloves provide excellent protection to metalworkers. Gloves can absorb cuts and burns, and can warn you of impending danger. Yet until a couple of years ago, I seldom wore gloves. I only donned gloves when I knew that I would exceed my pain threshold. Gloves were not so much protection as they were an extension of my working tolerances.

My reasoning was that I needed to feel what was going on—the processes of heating, forging, and grinding are all tactile as well as visual operations. Gloves do reduce your sensitivity. For this reason, I still do the final hollowgrind on a tool barehanded.

I want to know precisely how warm the tool becomes. But although gloves reduce sensitivity, they do not eliminate it. If anything, I am more sensitive to what I am doing because of the gloves. I know that they dull my sensitivity, therefore I anticipate more. I stay just ahead of problems.

Not all gloves are suitable for metalwork. I prefer welder's gloves, sometimes called gauntlets. The glove shells are leather, resistant to abrasion and lacerations. The linings of the gloves are cotton and provide good insulation from the leather, which tends to absorb and hold heat. When you fit yourself to a pair of gloves, be certain to get them large enough. These are not driving gloves. You should be able to remove either glove with a single quick fling of the arm. A glove heated to its burning point needs to be removed quickly and efficiently. Tight-fitting gloves could cause an accident they were intended to prevent.

CLOTHING

All clothing worn during metalwork ought to be cotton. Cotton only burns; man-made fibers melt into smoldering droplets. For added protection, wear a knee-length leather apron. Just brushing against a hot piece of steel sitting on the anvil—particularly at that height—is enough to ruin a day's forging. Wear sturdy shoes that aren't susceptible to meltdown.

FIRE EXTINGUISHERS

Fire extinguishers are a little like life preservers—a real bother to stow and maintain, but when you need one, nothing else will do. Most fires can be dispatched quickly and efficiently with the water you have on hand in the shop. And though I have never had an oil fire that was not containable in the oil bath can (remember the hinged lid), accidents do happen. Electrical fires are also a consideration. The $10 or $15 necessary to maintain a charged extinguisher is worth the peace of mind, even if you never use it.

A FINAL NOTE

Safety is not something you wear or a poster that hangs on the wall. The finest equipment in the world will not protect you absolutely. Safety has to be a part of how you work — an attitude. It has to be a sense of order that organizes the processes and allows you to focus on the work. Safety establishes the boundaries of caution that allow you that focus.

4

Beginning Projects

"Beginning," as in "Beginning Projects," should not be read to mean simple or easy. "Beginning," in this case, is really the transition between theory and application . . . between the armchair and the shop. This chapter is intended to provide a logical sampling of commonly used tools and introduce a variety of toolmaking procedures and techniques. These procedures and techniques are described in more detail here than they are in later chapters. Each beginning project focuses on a different set of procedures. Once a basic skill is mastered, you can more easily modify and incorporate it with other skills in making other tools—either from this book or from your own personal needs.

Finally, this chapter is intended as a reference. It is easy to get caught up in the heat of the forge and the beat of the anvil and to lose direction. "Beginning Projects" is here to refresh the memory and reestablish that direction.

Basic Forging and Heat Treatment: A Centerpunch

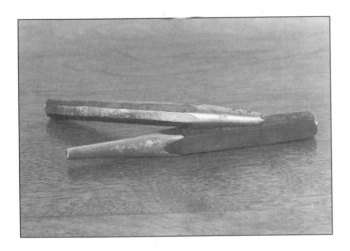

A centerpunch is used to punch a dimple in metal as a starting point for drilling a hole. The point of the punch is placed at the prospective hole site, and the head is struck with a hammer. The resultant dimple not only marks the location of the hole, but also helps to keep the drill from wandering, especially on smooth metal surfaces. Although a centerpunch may not be high on your tool priority list, it does serve as an excellent practice piece for four of the most basic toolmaking skills: forging, grinding, hardening, and tempering. You will also have an opportunity to use the tool when you begin making knives.

DESIGN

Like all tools, the centerpunch has certain design requirements, dictated by the function of the tool.

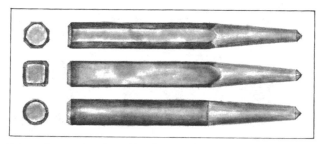

Octagonal, square, and round handles are all possibilities in this center-punch. The choice is yours.

A centerpunch has a point of about 90 degrees. That is, the point is a cone whose walls are sloped at about 45 degrees to the centerline of the tool. The punch tapers gradually over a distance of 1 to 3 inches (25 to 80 mm) from the handle to the point. The overall length of the tool ought to be 4 to 7 inches (100 to 180 mm). The head of the tool ought to be chamfered to control mushrooming during use. Beyond these very functional requirements, the tool is yours to design. The shape of the handle, the length of the taper, and the degree of finish are all yours to personalize.

I like a handle that has flat sides; the tool tends to stay put on the bench. For a first project, squaring a handle is probably enough of a challenge. Establishing a hexagonal or octagonal cross section is a bit more difficult, but that will come with time. You may prefer a round handle. You may elect to leave the hammermarks on the handle; the texture of rough forging will provide a good gripping surface. You may elect to smooth and polish the whole tool. As in any craft, these are all matters of choice and expression. They are what make a tool a personal article and not simply a thing of utility.

MATERIALS

Steel: Carbon steel (automobile coil springs are suggested), 4 to 7 inches (100 to 180 mm) long and ⅜ to ⅝ inch (10 to 16 mm) in diameter.

PROCEDURE

1. Straighten the stock. If you are using coil springs, straighten some stock by heating it in the forge and using pliers or Visegrips to pull out as much of the coil as you will need. At about a light orange color, the coil will open easily. Straighten only as much as you will need because coils are a handy storage format.

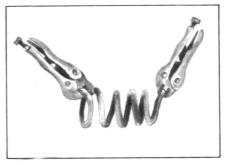

Automobile springs provide an excellent source of stock. Heat what you need to a light cherry red and then straighten.

2. Segment the stock. Once you have straightened as much stock as you will need, segment the steel using the cut-off hardy. When using the hardy, cut in almost halfway on opposing sides. Leave that last thin bit of connecting metal, and use the pliers to bend and fatigue the metal free from the coil. Cutting all the way through with the hardy would mean that you would be striking the cutting edge of the hardy with a hardened hammer face. This ruins the edge and means constant resharpening. Cutting all the way through may also result in launching the freed segment. You have enough to think about without having to consider the destination of some red-hot missile whose ballistics are uncertain. Bending the segment loose is much safer and requires little extra effort. If you don't have a hardy, heat the steel to a medium red after straightening, and bury it in the hot ashes. Allow it to cool slowly, annealing the metal. Segment it with a hacksaw later.

*Cut the stock **almost** through with the hardy. Finish the cut by bending the stock back and forth.*

3. Forge a straight blank. Forging lies somewhere between an artistic science and a scientific art. As this is your first project, you need to meet the requirements of both. Before you begin forging or shaping the punch, you need to true the blank. With a true, straight blank, all your work has a reference. You tend to wander less, and make fewer errors. Heat the blank to a light orange color. Let the high points of the blank stand above the anvil face and tap them down. Check the blank for alignment. Hold it out and rotate it so that you can see any irregularities in its axial rotation. After a few

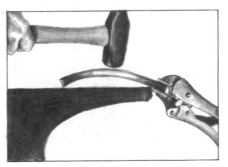

To true a blank, turn the bend away from the anvil and drive it down with the hammer.

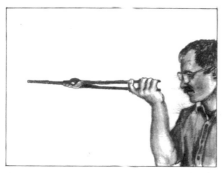

Check trueness by sighting down the blank and rotating it.

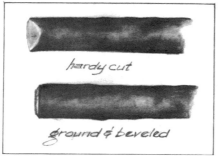

hardy cut

ground & beveled

A hardy cut is too crude for toolmaking. Grind it flat and bevel it to avoid folding during forging.

Establishing the flats requires more accuracy than power.

more corrective taps, observe again. Even though the punch is not a complex tool, forging with a true, straight blank is an important habit to develop.

4. Grind the ends flat. Once your stock is trued, look at the ends. When steel is hammer-forged, the outside of the material tends to move more than its core. This can cause folds at the ends of the work, which, if not corrected and forged into the matrix of the tool, will result in cracks. Although these cracks and folds may disappear during forging, they will reappear when you begin grinding and finishing the tool. To avoid the folding and the cracks, grind the ends flat. The steel will be annealed now so the grinding will only take a few minutes. First, grind the end flat and square to the long axis of the blank. Next, grind a 45-degree bevel that is 1/16 to 1/8 inch (2 to 3 mm) wide all around the end. This bevel will help compensate for the outer skin of your work moving faster than the core.

5. Flatten two opposing sides of the blank. With the blank trued and the ends beveled, you are now ready to begin forging. If you intend to forge flats on the handle, now is the time to do so. Whether the cross section is to be square, hexagonal, or octagonal, the process is the same. Bring the blank to a light orange color in the forge. Only that portion of the stock that you will be working needs to reach color. Using the tongs or Visegrips, hold the unheated end. Hold the steel cross-wise on the anvil, and run a line of overlapping hammerblows down its long axis. How hard to strike is dependent upon the weight of the hammer, the thickness of the blank, and the temperature reached. The result, however, should be a flat about 1/8 inch (3 mm) wide. This run of hammerblows is more or less replicated on the anvil side of the blank. The anvil side of the blank, however, will not produce a flat as wide as the hammer side. (The anvil works as a heat sink and cools the steel, reducing its movement.) To even the flats, rotate the blank 180 degrees and, using lighter blows, make the flat approximate its opposite. It is important to do this evening of opposite flats before proceeding to the next steps. Forging has to be balanced. If you maintain the balance as you progress, the work moves smoothly, quickly, and without aggravation. By making the small corrections, you avoid having to make the big corrections.

As this is probably your first experience at a forge, you will probably be out of heat by now. (Remember that if the steel has no glow, you are below the safe forging temperature. If you strike after the glow, you are likely to crack the blank. Even at a dull red, if you try to move the steel too rapidly, you are liable to produce cracks. And again, many of these cracks may not appear until you have invested time and energy in forging and have begun to finish the piece.) If you still have heat, take a moment to check the blank for trueness. If you are out of heat, do the straightening at the beginning of the next heat.

6. *Flatten remaining sides.* With two even flats established, your next hammerwork should be done 90 degrees to the established flats. It is the same process: a run of overlapping hammerblows followed by an evening of the anvil side of the blank. If you are making an octagonal handle, repeat this process twice more. A hexagonal cross section is a bit more difficult and requires that the second course of hammerblows be at about 60 degrees to the first set. A hex shape is probably a little advanced for a first project. It is more difficult to even out the flats and to keep the shape regular. Squares and octagons are almost self-regulating.

No matter the shape of the handle, the key to an even shape is allowing the flats to spread out slowly and evenly under the hammerblows. Let them grow until they just touch the adjacent flats. If you hurry

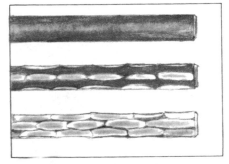

Develop the flats slowly, allowing them to emerge rather than forcing them. This calls for a light touch.

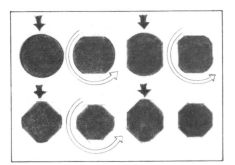

Forging an octagonal shape requires practice and patience. Be certain that opposite sides are even before rotating.

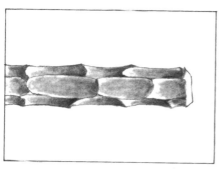

Although exaggerated here for emphasis, the hammermarks should just touch and produce even flats.

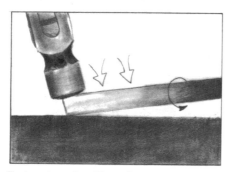

The taper is produced by angling the centerpunch handle above the anvil and working the heated area with the hammer as you rotate the blank.

the process, you produce irregularities: bulges, dips, and bends that are sometimes difficult to remove.

If you have elected a round handle that is textured rather than an angular shape, your hammerblows still ought to follow the long axis of the blank. The difference is that the flats are smaller and overlap one another. Done to perfection, the handle will appear to be shaped in hundreds of facets that are regular in shape and size.

7. Forge the taper. With the handle forged, you need to focus now on the taper and the point. Remember, the forging color is still light orange. Hammerblows on the taper should strike at an angle and the blank itself should be held at an angle of about 10 to 15 degrees to the anvil face. Do not worry about the exactness of the angle. If the angle is too great, the hammer will glance off the steel. If it is too slight, the blank will begin to flatten instead of taper. Work from the end of the blank back to the handle. Work all the way around the blank before moving up on the handle. Control the hammerwork. Overlap the hammermarks. Precise, controlled movements are more important than moving a great deal of metal. The taper should be delicate and appear to grow out of the handle. As you work up toward the handle, your blows should lighten. It may take half a dozen heats or more to develop this taper (at least in the beginning), and there are no rules that demand it sooner. Take your time. Check the blank regularly for trueness. Relax. Enjoy the work. Even after a lot of experience at the forge, it is easy to get caught up in the heat of the fire and the beat of the anvil. You try to extend your work beyond the safety of a forging heat. You become concerned with the quantity of hammerblows rather than quality. Take the time. Work with a rhythm that is comfortable. The tempo will increase as you develop the feel.

8. *Anneal.* As with other arts and crafts, an important aspect of forging is knowing when to stop. Overworking a piece can reverse your progress. Forging, at this point in your development, is not a finishing technique. Still, the more even and controlled your work is, the less you will have to do with the file and grinder. Eventually, you will produce forgings that are sufficiently refined at the anvil that they will require little or no refinement. These will be tools that not only show a mastery of technique, but also communicate a directness of intent that escapes many other crafts. The taper should stop when the end of the blank is about ⅛ to ³/₁₆ inch (2 to 3 mm) in diameter. Your last heat in the forge should be to a medium cherry red, and you should leave the steel in the hot coals to cool slowly as the fire dies down. This will anneal the steel and make the filing and grinding easier.

9. *Refine the handle.* I enjoy refining a steel shape. It is sculptural work. With a clear image of the tool in mind, your purpose is to help that shape emerge. Forging defined the shape, and now you need to refine it. Because the punch is a small tool, the file suggests itself as a direct yet sensitive method of refinement. (A grinder or a sander could be used, but I do not like working a small tool on these machines: it is too easy to overgrind; they are difficult to hold safely; the noise is too distracting for this delicate work.) Lock the punch horizontally in a vise. Leave enough of the punch above the surface of the jaws so that you have easy access. If you are cutting flats, use a double-cut, flat bastard file. Make your strokes with the file cut evenly all the way across the flat of the handle. Go easy at first. Get a feel for the metal removal. The blank will cut easily if it has been properly annealed. Keep your strokes flat and the surfaces will be flat. Repeat the process on each face until the handle is crisply defined. If a few hammerblows are much

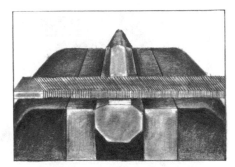

Lock the handle in the jaws of a machinist's vise. Then the flats can be evened with a file.

Smoothing the flats can be done with a flat hardwood stick wrapped with silicone carbide abrasive. Successively finer abrasives can produce an almost chrome look. The hardwood stick helps to keep the work crisp.

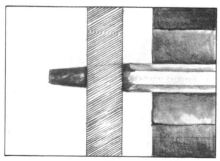

Smooth the taper first with a file and then, as with the flats, finish with silicon carbide paper.

deeper than the surface of the flat, you may want to consider leaving them. Aesthetically they may be a little objectionable. From a learning and developing standpoint, however, they will serve as a reminder that hammerwork requires more control than power. Once the handle faces are flat, even, and satisfactorily smooth, drawfile the surfaces with a single-cut, smooth file. Drawfiling should leave the surface smooth enough to sand with 220-grit, silicon carbide paper. Use a flat hardwood stick as support for the paper and a light oil as a lubricant. Work across the drawfile marks. (You work across the marks so that the deeper file marks will continue to show until they are removed.) Once the handle surfaces are flat, smooth, and even, you may want to soften the sharp edges. But go easy with the sandpaper. You want to remove only the sharpness, not the crispness.

If your punch is to have a round handle and maintain the hammermarks, use only the sandpaper. If there are some heavy marks that have sharp edges, you may want to do some localized filing. Use a less aggressive smooth file.

10. Refine the taper. Use a single-cut smooth file. Again, if some of the hammermarks are a little too coarse, you may want to use a coarser file locally to even them out. File first to even the taper, then drawfile to smooth. Use progressively lighter strokes.

If removing any hammermarks is not feasible— that is, if they are too deep—consider the overall design of the tool in shaping it. I personally do not see the marks of forging as detracting. Sometimes, in fact, especially where a surface need not be smooth, I like to leave the marks. The contrast between a refined, polished smoothness and the more direct but coarser forgework can be quite striking. Besides, this is your first project. You need to be a little reflective about it. If it is not perfect, you have still learned from it. Your next effort will be better for it.

11. Harden. The punch is now ready to be hardened. You do not grind the point now because it would be easily burned in the fire. Generally, cutting edges and points are cut after hardening. Place the punch in the fire pointfirst and in such a way that you may observe its entire length. Since the taper is the thinnest section, it will heat the quickest. You want a light cherry red color. If you have the fire burning too hot, it is difficult to observe the color of the heat. Let the steel heat slowly and evenly. Try not to stare into the fire. It will blind you to color changes—especially if the fire is too hot. Look away and look back. Observe dispassionately. When the color of heat is a light cherry red, remove the punch from the fire. (Hint: Before you remove the punch, be certain that your grips or tongs have a solid hold. Although this may seem obvious, it is easy to become overanxious at this point. Besides, you will need a good, solid grip to properly quench the tool.) Plunge the tool pointfirst into your brine quench. Plunge the tool in directly and keep it moving through the quench bath. For a small round tool like a punch, a back-and-forth motion is sufficient. For larger or more complex tools, tools that have irregular sides and sections, a figure-eight motion assures that the whole surface of the tool is being cooled equally. Keep the tool submerged for at least ten seconds. A larger tool would, of course, require more time and more motion in the bath.

12. Test for proper hardening. The punch should be cool to the touch before you remove it from the bath. The surface should be wet and shiny. If it dries quickly or is still steaming, resubmerge. Your first concern is to verify that you have obtained maximum hardness. With a sharp, preferably new, smooth file, attempt to file the taper of the

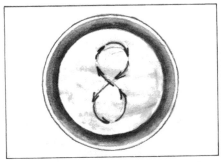

Because the shape of the centerpunch is nearly round, stirring a figure eight during the quench will produce an evenly hardened tool.

Make sure that the taper has hardened by drawing a new, sharp file across it. The file should not bite.

punch. If full hardness has been obtained, the file will glide over the surface without biting. It will remove the firescale from the surface, but it will not bite the metal. You will feel the difference if the punch has not been fully hardened. If you are not sure, use a magnifying glass to verify the absence (or presence) of file marks. If the punch has not been hardened, go back to the forge and bring the punch back up to temperature and quench again. If repeated attempts fail to fully harden the tool, you may have an alloy steel. Try an oil quench, and allow at least one minute for cooling. If oil fails, it may be an air-quench alloy. Allow the punch to cool in still air. If none of these remedies works and the spark test at the grinder still verifies the steel as a carbon steel, you probably have any of a number of exotic steels whose hardening instructions can only be guessed at. Automobile springs will invariably respond to the basic procedure: light cherry red, quench.

13. *Temper the handle.* With the punch hardened, you are close to completion. Your next major step is to temper the handle. Because the head will be struck with a hammer, you need to build some shock-absorption into the handle. Tempering will provide this shock absorption. Before tempering, however, you need to smooth and clean the surfaces to be tempered. Because temper colors are a result of surface oxidization, the surface must be smooth and free of rust inhibitors, such as the oil from your hands, in order to provide an accurate color indication. 220-grit paper followed by the buffer will smooth the surface. Methyl ethyl ketone (MEK) or denatured alcohol will then remove the buffing compound and fingerprints. With the surface smooth and free of oil you are ready to temper.

Because the punch is regular in cross section and because you will be tempering only a small amount of the handle, use the propane torch for tempering. A hot plate or even the forge could be used, but for such a small job they are not economical. Lock the taper end of the punch in a set of Visegrips firmly, but not so tightly that you mar the surface. Light the propane torch. (Be sure that its flame is clear of combustibles.) Since you are going to temper only the last inch or so of the punch handle, you should hold the head of the punch just at the edge of the propane's soft flame. Move the head in and out of the soft flame ½ inch (13 mm). Repeat the process a couple of times; let the heat equalize in the steel. Observe the surface of the punch in incandescent light. Look for color changes. Repeat the process.

It may take twenty passes before the first color changes appear. That first color will be a pale straw. The straw will deepen to a bronze and then to a brown. After the brown you'll see a red and a peacock color, followed by a purple and, finally, a blue. Blue is the temper color that you are after. But you only want the last 1 inch (25 mm) or so of the punch to be so tempered. If you heat the whole length of the punch, you would soften the whole tool. If you heat too slowly, the steel tends to conduct the heat equally throughout the length of the tool. If you heat too rapidly, the heat can build up and rush like a wave of color across the tool. In either event, it is prudent to have a bucket of plain water available to quench the tool before it is ruined. The punch point needs to remain fully hardened. If color runs to the point, you need to re-

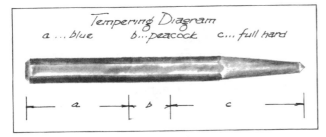

The tip and taper of the punch should not be tempered. Heat from the handle end first and allow the color to move toward the taper and point.

harden and then retemper. Again, removing the surface color does not change the temper of the tool.

Ideally, you will not have to quench to stop the color. Slowly and carefully build the heat and observe all the while. Develop a sense for how much heat is in the tool. Go through each sequence of color gradually so that you know where you are. (If you heat to a peacock, for example, and quench in a panic, you have to heat to beyond the peacock temperature before any change occurs. You lose your sense of timing.) Again, you stop at blue. Beyond blue and the color is a dead-looking gray — you have softened the steel too much. There will not be a clear line where the blue stops. There will, however, be a little rainbow of transition where the natural conductivity of the steel has carried the heat down further on the handle.

14. Grind the point. So far, you have forged the tool, refined its shape, polished, hardened, and tempered it. All that remains is to grind the point. Use a felt tip marker to mark a line on your grinder's work table that is 45 degrees to the face of the wheel. You will use this as a reference. Holding the punch flat on the table with one hand, smoothly and evenly rotate it with the other as the tool makes contact with the wheel. Very little pressure is required. Allow the wheel to cut. You do not want the point to heat to a tempering temperature. Because this is a localized grinding, if you rush it, the heat will not have a chance to dissipate through the rest of the tool, and you are liable to temper the point. Go slowly. Check the point for evenness. Check, too, for temperature build-up. Have plain water handy to quench. Be sure the stone is clean and freshly dressed. You want a perfect point. Take the time to be sure that the point is centered and even.

15. Test the centerpunch. Your first tool is done; try it out. Holding the punch vertical to a piece of

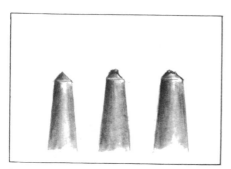

Use the grinder to set a 90-degree point. A reference line marked on the grinder's worktable will help you maintain the angle.

The final test is to use it. Left to right: good; too soft (if it was correct at the file testing, it may have been overheated during grinding); fractured (perhaps an imperfection in the forgework; check for cracks or folds).

mild steel, strike the head with a hammer. Check the steel. There should be a small crisp dimple in it. Now check the point of the punch. It should still be sharp. If it is not sharp or if it is bent, your angle is probably less than 45 degrees to the centerline of the punch (in other words, not a 90-degree point). Regrind. If the angles are correct and the punch dulls, the point was tempered somewhere along the process. If the file test after hardening accurately reflected full hardness, then you probably drew the temper during the grinding. Try grinding ⅛ inch (3 mm) off the taper, and reestablish the point.

Hollowgrinding and Heat Treatment: A Marking Knife

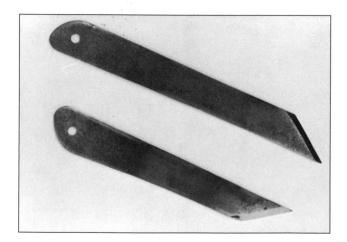

To precisely mark wood, no tool compares with the marking knife. The relatively fuzzy edge of a pencil line always leaves you with the question of exactly where to cut: which side of the line? When letting in a mortise, you wonder on which side of which line to place the chisel.

The marking knife is more direct. You sever the fibers of the wood with the knife. You have, in fact, started the cut. To start a chisel, you can actually feel when the position of the cutting edge is correct.

DESIGN

A marking knife may be nothing more than a blade, or it can be as complex and festooned as you care to make. I personally prefer the simplicity of a Japanese-style knife: a blade showing the nature of its origin and indicating its purpose. Since the blade is not intended for cutting, I do not handle the tool. Without a handle, I do not try to use it for cutting. This design is a safeguard for my weaker moments.

A marking knife has only a single bevel to its edge. The unbeveled, or backside, of the knife is held against a straightedge, ensuring that the knife follows the straightedge during marking without riding up, down, or into it. Because the marking knife is kept razor sharp, little pressure is required for it to cut or track properly.

MATERIALS

Steel: ¹/₁₆ to ⅛ inch x 1 to 2 inches x 6 to 8 inches (2 to 3 mm x 13 mm x 150 to 200 mm). A worn-out table saw blade, a used-up planer or jointer blade, or even a large coil spring section will do. You can forge the shape and thickness you need.

PROCEDURE

1. Prepare the stock. If your stock is from one of the woodworking blades, it will be even and flat, so you need only anneal the stock, scribe the pattern, and cut out the silhouette using a jeweler's saw. Remember that to anneal, you need to obtain a medium cherry red color and allow the steel to cool slowly.

If you have elected to forge the marking knife, either because you do not have the appropriate stock available or you are anxious to try your forging abilities, you must first prepare the stock by forging it into the appropriate format for shaping. This is probably one of the more rewarding approaches to making this tool. It demonstrates your ability to control shape, texture, and even finish at the forge. Remember during forging that the hammerwork should start at light orange and stop at

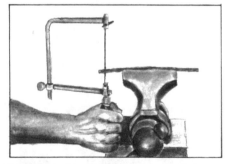

Once the stock has been annealed, a jeweler's saw can be used to silhouette the blade.

When forging a blade, make minor corrections for trueness as the need arises. If you make the little corrections, you will avoid the need to make the big corrections.

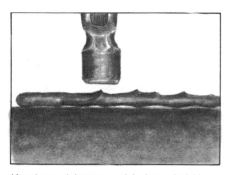

After the rough hammerwork is done, planishing will help refine the surface.

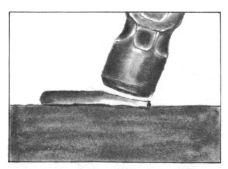

Forging the bevel not only saves time at the grinder, it may help the molecular arrangement at the edge. After the forging, check and correct the trueness.

dark cherry. Flatten the stock and even it out with the flat face of your largest cross or ball peen hammer. This is rough work and is intended to move the metal quickly. Leave the blank thicker than you will want the finished tool. With a lighter, more controllable hammer, flatten the stock. This is called *planishing*. The intent is to generally smooth the deeper, coarser hammermarks with lighter, controlled blows. For both the heavy and the light hammerwork, keep the same face of the stock to the anvil. This will require regular corrections, as the stock will want to curl away from the anvil. Simply flip the stock over and gently work the curve back. Avoid heavy corrective blows. You will want the back of this knife smooth, and any hammermarks will show as imperfections in your technique.

Once the stock is flat and planished evenly, you need to silhouette the knife. Anneal it first, then either use the jeweler's saw to cut to the scribed line, or if just a little metal needs to be removed, use the grinder. With the silhouette shaped, turn your attention to the cutting edge.

Beveling can be done at the forge as well. Using the lighter hammer, gently work out the area that will become a cutting edge, to no less than 1/16 inch (2 mm). The width of this bevel should be from 1/2 to 5/8 inch (13 to 16 mm) wide. Leave the bevel as smooth as possible.

At this point, both methods should yield a roughly shaped knife. Those who elected to use the forging technique have established a bevel. Even though those using flat stock could forge a bevel at this point, I do not recommend it. The stock is thin already, and forging the edge should leave it no less than 1/16 inch (2 mm).

2. Establish a hollowgrind. Establishing a hollowgrind at the grinder requires a frame of mind that is a little different from that of regrinding an established bevel. For an established bevel, you lock the worktable at the appropriate angle and maintain tool contact against the table constantly. The table is the reference. Because your stock for this project is probably too small to obtain the slight angle of 25 degrees while keeping the tool on the table, establishing the hollowgrind will require you to freehand the shape on the grinder. Although this sounds nervy, the technique and skill, once developed, are very useful. You will be working the wheel above the equator. This is usually a "Don't." With the prohibition clearly in mind and your sensibilities consequently heightened, you will still need to proceed with caution.

When hollowgrinding any tool edge, use your hands to "jig" the blade.

With the bevel side down against the wheel, you have to imagine the path that the wheel will cut and how your hands will need to move in order to cut the path where you want it. Your grip needs to be firm and fluid. The pressure against the wheel is light—just enough to keep it from bouncing but not so tight as to cause the wheel to dig into the steel. Control, not pressure, is the goal. Touch the blade to the spinning wheel. Just touch. Observe the mark the wheel made. Adjust accordingly. Touch the blade to the wheel again. Observe the mark. Adjust. When you have the wheel marking the bevel at about ⅛ to ³/₁₆ inch (3 to 5 mm) back from the cutting edge, you have found the proper location for the hollowgrind. Test the marks at different locations along the cutting edge.

Use a delicate touch when hollowgrinding and keep the tool moving.

Once you have a good sense of the wheel's path, you are ready to establish the hollowgrind. The pressure remains light. Let the wheel cut a hollow without moving the blade. It should be a slight hollow—just enough that the wheel can register on it. Stop the grinder. Try to register the hollow against the wheel without looking. Try this registration process with the grinder on. Once you feel comfortable with it, widen the hollow slightly and inspect. Usually, you will find that the hollow remains parallel to the cutting edge. Continue to widen the

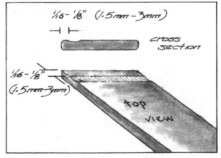

Because this tool is thin in cross section, just start the hollowgrind. If it is ground too thin, it may be ruined during the hardening process.

hollowgrind until it is established along the edge. Most of this technique is a matter of visualization. By observing from the side opposite the action, you are able to predict the result. It is not too different from installing a screw in an inaccessible location. You look at the actual location, if you can, or feel with your fingertip for the hole. You adjust your alignment accordingly. Usually you are successful. It is really no different when grinding. In fact, it is somewhat easier because you can observe the opposite side directly. Your brain and hands adjust almost subconsciously.

(Note: This method of grinding is safe as long as you remain alert to what you are doing. Use a good grinder with a freshly dressed wheel and only slight pressure. Applying heavier pressure diminishes your control. As your control fails, you compensate by gripping harder. You lose more control. You may push the edge of the tool into the wheel. Given a good bite at the tool, the wheel will throw the knife down against the worktable or into your apron. Visualization and control are the key to success.)

Your hollowgrind is established when you have a continuous, even grind that will be easy to register against the wheel after hardening.

3. *Smooth.* You have shaped and beveled the tool and established the hollowgrind. For those who have chosen to use flat stock, you are ready to prepare your steel for hardening and tempering. Both sides of the knife need to be smoothed to at least 220-grit before hardening. After hardening, it will need to be smoothed to 400-grit, buffed, cleaned, and tempered.

Those of you who have elected to forge your knives have another step to take. You have worked hard to produce a satisfactory hammerfinish on this tool. If the work went well and you like its appearance, you are probably reluctant to polish away that surface work. You do not have to. First, however, you do need to flatten the back of the knife and smooth it to at least 220-grit. Drawfiling will do the rough flattening. Progressively finer grits of abrasive paper will finish the job nicely. Keep the knife flat. Rounding the edges over now will mean more work later, at the benchstone. Leave the face of the knife as it came from the forge. The polished back of the knife will provide the clean surface you need to observe the color transformation during tempering.

4. *Harden and temper.* Both the cut knives and the forged knives are ready for heat treatment: hardening and tempering. The quench should be oil, because a brine quench is too violent for the thinness of a knife. Cracking, or at least warping, would be the probable consequence. Heat the whole tool to a light cherry red. Hold the knife parallel and perpendicular to the surface of the oil. Submerge it quickly and cleanly into the bath. The objective is to cool all the surfaces of the steel as evenly and simultaneously as possible. Unlike a brine quench, where you use a figure-eight pattern to promote cooling, you should only move the knife up and down, perpendicular to the surface. In doing so, you sacrifice a little hardness and a little depth of case. What you gain is a tool that is sufficiently hard and free of cracks and distortions. Keep the tool submerged for at least one full minute. Use the file test to verify hardening.

5. *Polish to prepare for tempering.* The combination of a thin cross section and full hardness means that your knife is relatively fragile at this point. If dropped—even to a wooden floor—it might shatter. Tempering has to be the next step. With this fragility in mind, prepare the knife for tempering. The extra step of flattening the back of the forged blade now means that those who have been using the forging technique have only the flat of the back to polish. A fine wire wheel is about all that is necessary for removing the firescale from the bevel side of the blade.

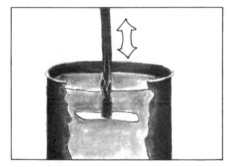

Submerge the blade in an oil quench to harden it. Since it is flat, use only an up-and-down motion. Figure eights might cause uneven cooling and warp the blade.

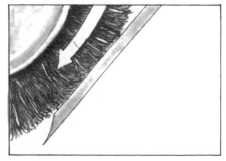

A wire wheel can be used to remove firescale without removing the hammermarks. Use the wheel as you would a buffer and work only below the equator.

6. Temper. Tempering a knife blade is a little like painting a watercolor landscape. You start with the blue sky and wash the color lighter as it approaches the horizon. The sky in this case is the spine and handle of the knife. Instead of pigment, you use heat. The colors, however, are the same. I use my propane torch for tempering knives. Because I can observe the flame, I have some sense of how directly the heat is being applied.

Start at the handle. Holding the back edge of the handle at about 1 inch (25 mm) from the observable flame, move the knife back and forth in the heat, not allowing the heat to focus in any one area. After two or three passes at just the handle edge, allow the spine of the blade to pass through. For those with the forged blades, this will be the only area that shows color. Be sure that you can observe the polished surface of the back.

Keep this pattern of movement going. Your objective will be to have a blue handle, a vermilion-peacock spine, and a straw cutting edge. A greater amount of heat is required for the larger mass of the handle to obtain blue. A lesser amount is required for the smaller mass of the blade and its lesser temper color (vermilion). The least amount of heat is required for the cutting edge, which is tempered the least (straw) and has the slightest mass. Do not be tempted by the slowness of the straw to appear to make a fast pass of the cutting edge directly through the heat. There is sufficient heat building in that spine. It will be conducted through the steel down into the cutting edge. That tempering color may, if you are not patient, wash with sickening speed to blue at the thinnest section of the cutting edge.

7. Finish the hollowgrind. With tempering complete, you are ready to finish the hollowgrind. Use the referencing method you used before at the grinder. You need to be mindful of heat created by the grinder. The wheel should be freshly dressed.

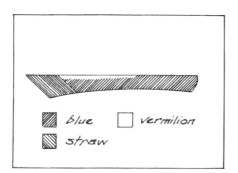

Temper the handle to blue and the cutting end to straw. The thin line of red or vermilion theoretically adds a little extra rigidity.

The pressure should be light enough that the tool does not become too hot to handle. Have plain water handy to quench, but try to control the temperature by reducing pressure. The hollowgrind is complete when you produce a burr on the backside of the knife. Hone both the bevel and the back of the knife.

Handle-ing a Tanged Tool: A Screwdriver

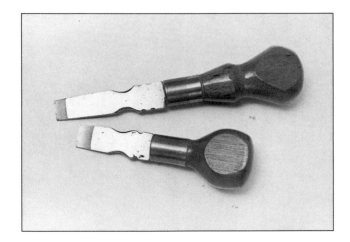

Along with hammers, pliers, and coat hangers, screwdrivers are in that category of universal, multipurpose tools that are seldom exactly suited to the task at hand, but get the job done . . . sort of. From a design standpoint, the greatest fault of most screwdrivers is that the blade is too thin to lock into the slot. Because the undersized blade has only two small areas in contact with the slot, the harder steel of the driver distorts the screwslot.

DESIGN

This screwdriver is designed specifically for tightening the large standard screw that locks the chipbreaker to the blade on double-iron planes. It is made to fit the slot. Although this may seem to be too limited an application for the two hours it will

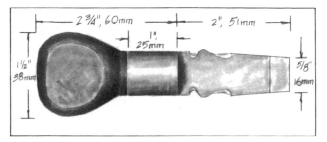

The dimensions of a screwdriver for tightening the large screw in double-iron planes.

take you to make the screwdriver, there is an indescribable satisfaction in using a tool perfectly matched to its task. This is also a good first project requiring the handle-ing of a tanged tool.

Because the chipbreaker's locking screw is normally tightened by holding the irons in one hand and torquing the driver with the other, the driver shaft is better short than long. (Besides, the greater torque of a long shaft is not necessary.) This tool is a little longer than what is called a stubby, but shorter than a standard screwdriver. The detail on the shaft is borrowed from the last century, when tools had a design beyond function. The handle is large and comfortable and provides a steady, even grip.

You can take advantage of the brittle nature of fully hardened steel and break a file where it is supported in the vise jaws. Be sure to drape the file with cloth to protect yourself against chips. (Drape is not shown for clarity.)

MATERIALS

Steel: An old flat file of appropriate size or other suitably sized stock.

Ferrule: ⅝-inch (16-mm) I.D. brass or copper tubing. Pneumatic hose repair couplings (brass usually) work well also.

Handle: Hardwood stock.

PROCEDURE

1. Anneal or normalize the stock. An alternative to firing up the forge for this project is to normalize with the oxyacetylene torch. Normalizing is not absolutely necessary, but it makes the job easier and allows for the use of a variety of shaping tools.

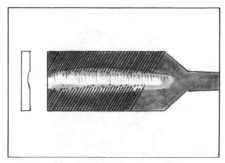

Files are an excellent source of steel. Before forging, however, the teeth of the file must be removed. The first path of the grinder is shown here.

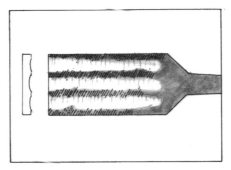

The second and third passes at the grinder should be even with and parallel to the first pass.

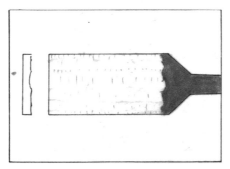

The third series of passes, depending on the size of the file, should remove any of the remaining cusps.

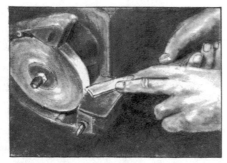

Silhouetting the screwdriver blade is light work and can be done most easily at the grinder.

2. *Cut the blank to rough length.* If you're using an old file, cut from the end with the tang; it will save you from having to grind one later. Cutting can be done with an abrasive cut-off wheel, with a cutting torch (leave ¼ inch (6 mm) extra to remove the slag of cutting), or with a hacksaw if you have annealed. An alternative method, if you haven't normalized, is to break the file in a vise with a hammer. Be sure to have your safety glasses on *and* shroud the file with a cloth. Strike the file as close to the jaw's grip as possible. Because files are generally untempered martensite, they are very brittle and usually respond to this method. Do not use your hands; the steel will have a number of internal stress cracks that may not be visible. If it breaks in your hand, it may offer shards to your palm.

3. *Remove the file teeth.* With the blank cut to rough length, the next step is to remove the file teeth. While this step may seem merely cosmetic, it is important to the structure of the tool as well. If left on the steel, the teeth may, during hardening, set up lines of stress and failure. If you have annealed, a file will remove the teeth nicely. Begin with a coarse-cut, and finish with a smooth-cut file.

If the material has not been annealed, use the grinder. Begin by grinding a furrow in the center of the long axis of the stock, the center of which just removes the teeth. Grind successive parallel furrows nearer the outer edges. Leave these edges. They will serve as guides to keep the sides parallel. Use a disk sander or a belt sander to flatten the furrows. Hold the tang with locking pliers. Don't use your hands for pressure on the back; use a push stick.

4. *Scribe the shape of the blade and tang and grind to shape.* With the teeth removed and the broad faces still parallel, scribe the blade and shaft design on the blank. Grind just to the line. Leave the width of the line to remove with subsequent abrasives. When grinding a tool as small as this, I don't wear gloves. It is too easy to lose the feel and control of the grinding. Using your bare hands will require you to make frequent coolings in a bucket of water.

Take your time grinding. Use even-pressured strokes that utilize the entire grinding surface. The heat builds quickly. Dip the piece in the water often. If the heat causes you to let go of the blank, it may become caught between the rest and the wheel, be sucked into the shrouding, or be ejected. None are pleasant. Be safe. Quench often.

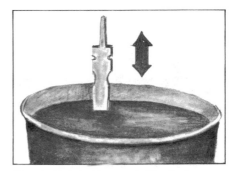

Since the blade is thin, quench it in oil using an up-and-down motion. The tip should enter first.

The grinder will work well for all of the edge work except for squaring the shoulders of the tang. If the blank has been annealed, a flat square file is the best tool. Grind as close as you can and square the shoulders with the file. If the blank is still hardened, you can use the abrasive cut-off wheel to nibble at the shoulders. Raise the wheel as high as it will go. With a new wheel, this will make the cuts nearly square with the faces of the blade. Avoid the temptation to use side pressure on the wheel. The nibble marks can be removed after hardening and tempering.

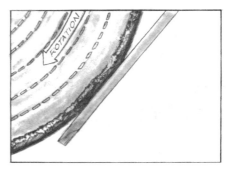

Polishing the blade after hardening is necessary in order to read the temper colors properly. Keep the blade below the equator when buffing.

Grinding the hollows into the edge of the blade is optional. This little bit of design, while not functional in the truest sense, adds a little personalization to the tool. A small grinding wheel chucked in a drill press will do this nicely.

5. Smooth the surfaces. After cutting and shaping the blade, smooth the whole surface. Depending on how clean your heat source for hardening is, you may want to polish it. In any event, the cleaner and smoother the tool is before hardening, the less work you will have to do after hardening.

6. Harden. Heat the blade in the forge to 1,475°F (826°C) so the steel is a medium cherry red. As the tool is thin in section, use an oil bath for quenching. Be certain to keep the tool in the oil for at least 90 seconds. Oil cools much more slowly than

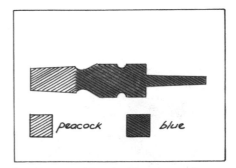

Because a screwdriver should not damage the head of the screw, screwdrivers are tempered softer than cutting tools. Apply the heat to the tang end of the tool and allow the color to spread forward.

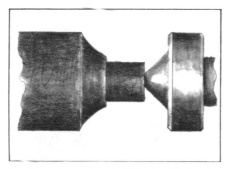

Turn the neck area down to fit the handle's ferrule. It should be a snug fit.

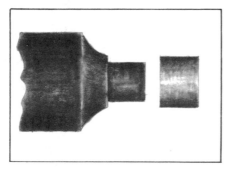

Demount the turning, fit the ferrule, and remount the whole assembly.

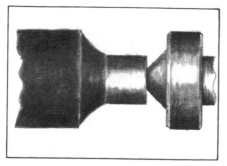

With the ferrule mounted, flush the handle to the ferrule.

brine. Removing it from the bath too early will reduce the depth of case or worse still, temper itself out of hardness.

7. *Clean and polish.* After hardening, clean and polish the tool. Wash it thoroughly after polishing and just before tempering.

8. *Temper.* Temper the blade at the tip section to blue and at the upper part of the blade near the tang, to peacock.

HANDLE-ING

Handles ought to complement the tools they serve. A well-designed handle increases the utility of the tool. If the tool is a struck tool, such as a chisel, the handle ought to be easy to hold and tough enough to resist repeated blows. If it is a tool that is subjected to torque, such as a screwdriver, the handle needs to facilitate not only the grip, but the torquing motion as well.

Due to the very specific use of this tool, the amount of torque required is minimal. As such, the primary criterion for the handle is that it be comfortable and easy to use. Probably the easiest way to tighten the screw of a chipbreaker is with a palm grip: The handle is centered in the palm and the fingers close on the handle as in making a fist. With the elbow and wrist locked, the articulation is at the shoulder. It is a short but powerful and easily controlled motion.

The handle for such a motion ought to be large enough to fit the palm but small enough to be gripped solidly by the fingers. Experiment in clay. Grip the clay as though you were using it as the tool. Watch what your hands do to the clay. Observe the impressions. They will suggest shapes that are specific to you and your grip.

Turning a handle. Turning is the easiest and quickest way to start a handle. The lathe produces a round, symmetrical shape that can be modified with other tools to suit the need.

As shown in the illustration, turn the handle with the ferrule end mounted to the dead center of the lathe. Turn the neck of the handle down to fit snugly inside the ferrule. Once the ferrule fits, mount it on the blank. Turning the rest of the handle with the ferrule in place will make it easier to blend the ferrule into the design. It is also easy to smooth and polish the ferrule on the lathe.

For a more finished look, you may want to make a longer ferrule and "neck down" the end with a burnisher. The burnisher ought to be a smooth, round-nosed piece of steel that is long enough to allow for the safe use of the tool rest. By applying pressure with the burnisher, the softer ferrule may be moved inward to close around the tip of the dead center. This necking down is limited to ferrules made of copper or brass. Before mounting the ferrule, anneal it with the propane torch. Both copper and brass are annealed by heating to a red color. Brass can be made softer still by quenching (in plain water) from the red color. When the handle is finished and removed from the lathe, cut a slot in the necked-down section of the ferrule to accept and conceal the shoulders of the screwdriver blade.

Carving a handle. Handlemaking does not have to be limited to the lathe. In fact, some handles are better carved.

Begin with stock that is longer than you need. The extra length allows you to secure it in a vise. Rough out the shape of the handle using a gouge. Once the rough shape is established, refine it using rasps and files or sandpaper. I prefer to work it with a small carving knife after the gouge work. It is a very direct way to work. It also leaves a finely faceted surface that is both aesthetically pleasing and easy to grip. With a little practice, it should take no longer to carve a handle than to turn one.

Mounting the handle. Mounting the screwdriver blade in the handle is relatively straightforward. Drill a hole in the center of the handle that is in

With a round-tip burnisher, burnish the end of the ferrule over the end of the wood.

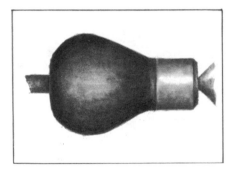

Finish the rest of the handle.

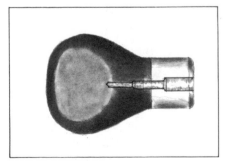

Mounting the tapered tang in the handle requires a stepped hole. Drill the minor diameter first.

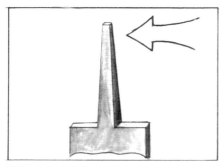

Heat only the last ¼ inch (6 mm) to a dull cherry red.

Do not drive the handle on all the way. Leave about ⅛ inch of tang unseated. Allow it to cool for a full 10 seconds.

After the pause, drive the handle home with a mallet. This last little movement should put the tang into fresh, unburned wood and hold the blade securely. If it is loose, use epoxy to fix the blade in position.

line with the axis of the handle and is a little smaller than the tang—small enough that the tang could be driven into the handle with light tapping from a mallet, but not pushed in by hand. If the tang has a sharp taper, you may need to drill a succession of gradually larger and shallower holes to accommodate both the point of the tang and its major width near the shoulders. Still, because you cannot make a dry run of mounting, the hole has to be an estimate.

With the hole drilled in the handle, lock the driver blade in your vise. (Use soft jaws or a wood vise to avoid scarring the blade.) Heat the tang from its point downward about ¼ inch (6 mm) to a dull cherry red with a propane torch. Immediately—before the heat dissipates—take the handle, align it with the blade (traditionally any flats on the handle are aligned parallel to the flat of the blade) and push the handle onto the blade. If you cannot push it to within ⅛ inch (3 mm) of full seating (shoulders touching ferrule), use a mallet to tap it the rest of the way. In either case, stop short of full seating. There will be hissing and smoke exiting from the hole in the hardening. This is as it should be. Let the handle stay that last ⅛ inch (3 mm) away from full seating for about ten seconds. Then tap it forward to full seat. This pause allows gas to escape, and the subsequent tapping will make the tang seat in fresh, unburnt wood, thus providing a stronger mounting. This should provide a solid lock between handle and blade that will last the life of the tool.

If the handle is loose, or works loose, use epoxy. Fill the hole with epoxy and drive the blade into the handle. Use acetone or MEK to clean up the overflow.

Handle-ing with Slabs: A Utility Knife

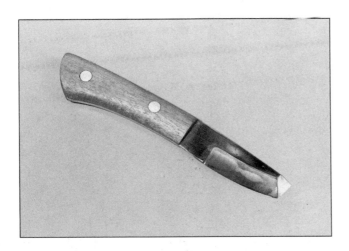

I use few tools with more regularity than my utility knife. It sits on a small shelf above my bench with a small square, a 6-inch (150-mm) steel scale, a small hand lens, and my favorite polishing plane. While my other tools all have specific purposes, the utility knife is there to serve any of a hundred different needs. It has cut strapping, PVC, thin sections of brass and copper, a nail (once on a bet), and dried glue. It has scraped gaskets, glue, and epoxy; stripped wire; removed slivers; and pried brads straight. It has even, on occasion, cut wood. When the instructions direct you to "take an old chisel," reach for this utility knife.

DESIGN

Like any good tool, the design of this one has evolved over the years. My first utility knife had a regular point with a slightly dropped edge and was probably half again as large as the current design. A point is a necessity, but the point on a utility knife needs to be rugged. A long, relatively slender point will break with abuse. And finally, a utility knife should have an edge that is more tough than sharp. (Cutting wire and dried epoxy requires toughness.) And as it frequently is used as a chisel, it should have a single bevel. The result is not a particularly graceful or elegant-looking tool. Its real beauty lies in its utility.

MATERIALS

Steel: ⅛ x 1 x 6 inches (3 x 25 x 150 mm). Saw blades, jointer or planer blades, or thin auto leaf springs are all satisfactory.

Wood: Handle slab material. (Any hardwood that you will be comfortable living with for the next decade or so.)

Pins: ⅛ to ¼ inch (3 to 6 mm) brass wire. (Brazing rod works well and is readily available.)

Epoxy: I use five-minute epoxy because I am always in a hurry.

PROCEDURE

1. *Design the handle shape.* All tools are better designed and made when the craftsman who will use them is also the toolmaker. The design of this knife works well for me, but I have large palms and relatively stubby fingers. Your knife ought to fit your hands. Take a few moments to experiment with some shapes in pine. Remember that this will be a multipurpose tool, and avoid aligning the grip to any specific purpose. At the same time, the handle needs to be comfortable and workable for most any use. A few minutes of experimentation and discovery, and the handle will design itself. At the risk of sounding too Californian, "go with the flow" is sound advice for handle design.

2. *Anneal the stock.* Annealing allows you to cut the carbon steel stock with a hacksaw or jeweler's saw. Remember, heat to a medium cherry red and cool slowly . . . the slower the better.

3. *Prepare the blank.* Transfer the pattern to the steel, and cut out the profile. Grind and file the blank smooth. While the outside radii of the profile are easily ground, you may, depending on your handle design, need a half-round file for the inside radii. Be sure to flatten and smooth the edge of the blank. A *slight* softening of all the sharp edges is a good safety measure. Even a 90-degree edge can cut if squeezed a little too enthusiastically. This smoothing of the edges is not finish work. You will finish the edges after hardening, tempering, and handle-mounting. Your objective at this point is a safe, comfortable workpiece.

4. *Drill the pinholes.* With the tool cut to its profile, focus on the handle area for a moment. In addition to epoxy, the handle slabs will be held to the tang by two brass pins. Because the steel is annealed, this is a good time to locate and drill the pinholes. To locate the pinholes, you need to consider the nature of the wood that will be pinned to the tang. The pins should be no closer than ½ inch (13 mm) from the ends of the wood. Closer to the ends, and many woods will split, either when you drive the pins through or afterward, when you mushroom the heads. Locate the holes and, using the centerpunch you made earlier, centerpunch the hole sites.

Boring into metal requires more caution than does boring into wood. Clamp the blank to a piece of hardwood and secure the blank and the backup board to the table. If the steel blank is not locked solidly in place, vibration could move it during boring. If the piece moves, it could lock on the drill bit, raising the blank and the board off the table as it spins all the while. (Without the backup board you could have only the blade spinning like a dull

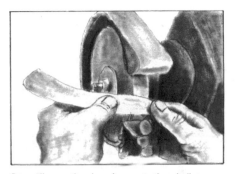

Depending on the size of your stock, grinding may be easier and faster than sawing. Take your time grinding. Although the metal has been annealed and a build-up of heat will do no metallurgical harm, holding a hot piece of metal while grinding isn't safe. Quench frequently.

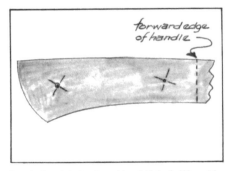

Locate the pinhole sites at least ½ inch (13mm) in from the ends of the handle.

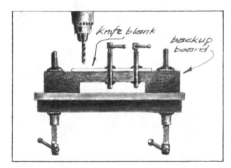

Whenever you bore into metal, take the time to secure the work. Knife blanks in particular are dangerous if the bit locks into the work and the blank rises, spinning and slashing.

The knife blank, already drilled for pinholes, makes the perfect template for drilling the handle slabs. Again, be sure to secure your work.

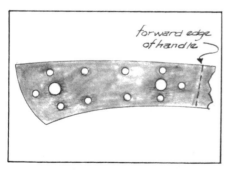

Once you have drilled the large holes for the pins, locate and drill the epoxy rivet holes. The epoxy will flow through these holes and harden into rivets. Epoxy rivet holes should be about ⅛ inch (3mm) in diameter.

but effective scythe.) An extra minute or two to secure things properly is worth the investment. Select a bit that is about ¹⁄₆₄ inch (.5 mm) larger than the diameter of the pin material and drill at the slowest speed setting on your drill press (down to 200 rpm).

5. *Locate and drill the holes in the handle slabs.* While you are still set up, you should drill the pin-holes through each handle half. At this point, the two slabs should only be roughly shaped, but their inside surfaces should be flat and true. The steel blank makes an excellent template. Simply clamp the slab to the blank and clamp both to a backup board. Align the drill bit with the first hole, then secure the backup board, slab, and blank to the table before drilling. (Do not start the drill motor with the bit in the hole. It would probably bind.) When you've drilled both holes in one slab, mark it either right or left so that later on you'll have a reference for how this slab fits to the tang. Be sure that when you drill the second set of pinholes, you drill from the opposite side of the template. Handle slabs are left- and right-handed.

6. *Drill epoxy rivet holes.* In addition to the brass pins, epoxy is used to keep the slabs attached to the tang. To maximize the epoxy's adhesion, drill several small holes through the tang. When the slabs have been mounted and the epoxy is dry, these holes will be filled with what amounts to epoxy rivets, providing continuous adhesion to both slabs through the tang. These holes ought be about ⅛ inch (3 mm) in diameter. Two or three holes around each of the brass pinholes and a few in the center will provide more than adequate holding power . . . even for a utility knife.

7. *Establish the hollowgrind on the blade.* Use the method that you used on the marking knife. Remember, only establish the hollowgrind now. Leave at least ¹⁄₁₆ inch (2 mm) of metal at the edge. The angle of the edge for this sort of tool ought be no slighter than 30 degrees. A delicate edge has no place on this knife.

8. Harden. Smooth the blank to 220-grit, heat to light cherry red, and quench in oil. If this is the only project you are working on, you may want to use the oxyacetelyne torch for obtaining color. If you do use the torch, try to focus your eyes on the knife and away from the torch flame. The torch may blind you to, or lessen your perception of, color changes in the blank. Also, be sure to extinguish the flame before quenching. Depending on the type of oil you're using in your quench and its vapor volatility, you do not want to mix the two. After quenching, verify hardness with the file test.

9. Smooth and polish the blank, then temper. Remember that before the blank has been tempered, it is brittle and therefore fragile. Temper the handle blue, the spine vermilion, and most of the blade a strong straw color. The darker straw color is a little softer and more resilient than I usually use on a woodcutting edge. The abuse that the knife is put to, however, demands a more resilient blade.

10. Finish the hollowgrind, then hone. Both grinding the hollowgrind and honing are more easily accomplished before the handle slabs are mounted.

11. Mount the handle. This part of the procedure is generally the messiest and sometimes the most frustrating. Pins roll away, handles get reversed, and the phone rings. Take the time to do a dry fit-up. As in woodworking, most major surprises can be avoided during assembly if you take the time to fit everything together dry. Include the clamps during the fit-up. Have paper towels and solvent handy for cleanup. Do not fit the actual pins. If the holes are good and snug, removing them may damage the slab material. Use some undersize pins to verify alignment.

After the dry fit-up, prepare the mating surfaces for the epoxy. The oil in your hands will provide

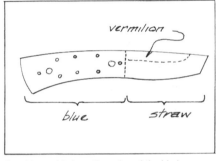

As with most knives, the spine of the blade should be vermilion and the rest of the blade straw. The tang should be blue to absorb shock.

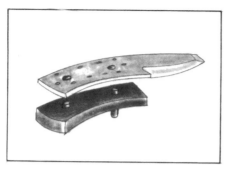

After applying epoxy to both mating surfaces, push the pins through the slab far enough so that they will just pass through the tang. When the opposite slab and tang surfaces have been prepared, the slightly protruding pins will help index the handle into location.

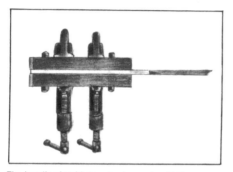

The handle should remain clamped until the epoxy is thoroughly cured. While the epoxy is still soft, clean up the squeeze-out with acetone.

somewhat of a barrier to the epoxy, so wash the tang in MEK, and either wear rubber gloves or avoid touching the surfaces. If you are using an exotic wood for the handle, wash the mating surfaces of the slabs. Prepare your epoxy. Choose one side of the handle to work from, and fit the pins into the slab. Allow them to protrude about $1/16$ inch (2 mm) through the outside surface. Coat the mating surface of this slab with epoxy. Coat it evenly but not too thickly (presuming that these are two flat and parallel surfaces, there will not be much room for epoxy). Next, coat the matching side of the tang. Align the pins to the pinholes in the tang and press the two together evenly. The trick is to keep the two surfaces parallel; they only need to touch one another. Coat the other side of the tang with epoxy. This time, be sure that the epoxy rivet holes are filled. Spread epoxy to the other handle slab and, aligning with the pins, press this second slab into position. Clamp it and clean up. In addition to my hands, apron, pants and shirt, the bench, the floor, and the clamps, I usually wipe up any squeeze-out that is on the tool itself. Be sure that the pins protrude from both sides of the handle. If not, tap them gently until they do.

12. Shape the handle and finish. Some will choose to file the shape. Others will carve it. Still others will use power abrasives. All are reasonable methods. The only caution is to not overspecialize the handle. Finger holds that can be used from only one position diminish the tool's capabilities.

Leave $1/32$ inch (1 mm) of the pin protruding from either side. When you have the handle down to its final thickness, peen both ends of the pins. Set one end of the pin on a rigid, hard surface and, using a small hammer, gently tap the other end. Turn the knife over and peen the other side. The pins will mushroom slightly and lock the handle into position.

Use tung oil as a finish. Thin the first coat to about half oil and half thinner. This is a soak coat. Let it dry a day or two. The second coat is applied full strength, allowed to sit until tacky, and then rubbed vigorously. Allow this coat to dry for at least two days, then buff it. (I save one buffing wheel just for polishing handles.) Buff lightly without lingering in one spot for too long. The result is a warm, burnished glow.

5

Chisels

If you have completed the first four projects in this book, you have now learned most of the basic toolmaking procedures. The instructions have been detailed to provide a logical, organized, and complete progression. For the projects that follow, only the new techniques and special considerations will be given the same in-depth explanation. Use Chapter 4 as a reference if you need a reminder on how to accomplish some procedure or technique.

A General-Purpose Chisel

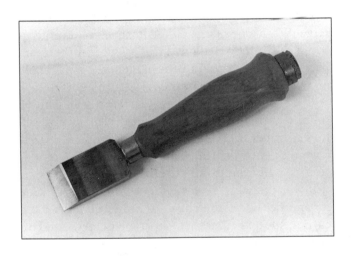

Years ago, when I began woodworking seriously, many of my tools were purchased secondhand; some were even antiques. Their age was not so much a function of nostalgia as a matter of economics. Flea market and garage sale prices were much more reasonable than buying new. In my assortment of several dozen chisels, there were samples of all types: straight- and bevel-sided; wood-, plastic-, and even steel-handled; socket- and tang-style shanks; thick-bladed, thin-bladed, and in several cases, some blades that were lopsided in cross section. In short, there was a great variety that touched on about every design and flaw.

For general use, for small, controlled cuts, for paring small parts, for about everything that we look to a common, garden-variety chisel to do, I came to prefer chisels that had been almost used up. With blade lengths of only 1 to 1½ inches (25 to 40 mm), these were chisels that I had initially relegated to the spare parts drawer. There didn't seem to be enough left of these chisels to bother with sharpening and honing. At some point I needed an odd-sized chisel to inlet several dozen odd-sized butt hinges. The stop cut needed to be $5/16$ inch (8 mm) wide. The ¼-inch (6-mm) chisel was too small for a single cut, the ⅜-inch (10-mm) too large. While considering the alternatives, I remembered the stubby remains I had stowed in the spare parts drawer. I reground the 1-inch (25-mm) blade of what had been a ⅜-inch (10-mm) chisel to a width of $5/16$ inch (8 mm). As usual, I was in a hurry to finish the project. The work went well; the hinges fit perfectly. I may have been impressed that I would finish on time, but there were no revelations, no lightbulbs of "eureka!"

It was probably a year later, when I was looking for another odd-sized chisel, that I remembered my earlier success. Another short blade reground to size, sharpened, and honed; another success. Finally, a dim flicker of light began to penetrate the haze. By then I had done some toolmaking a la Alexander Weygers and his books. I had even made a few chisels. But up to this point, my chisels had merely followed the pattern of manufactured chisels. Long-bladed and heavy, these chisels were no better than their commercial brethren, only cheaper.

For the sake of your own personal revelation, try this: Take a long-bladed chisel, and while holding it by the handle, move it to a scribed mark. How easy was it to move it to the mark? Now try it again, only this time relax. Hold the chisel any way you want to, and move it precisely to the mark. Notice where your hand moves—down the handle and onto the blade. Most of us do this without thinking. It's natural. You need the proximity to the cutting edge for control.

Using a typical chisel. A small movement at the wrist becomes a large movement at the blade tip.

A shorter chisel reduces the arc.

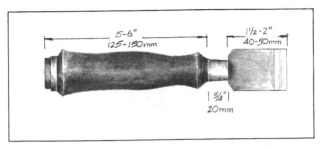

The dimensions of a Bench Chisel. Not only does the shorter blade respond more directly to wrist movement, but with the weight of the tool well forward, the tool seems to have better balance as well.

DESIGN

The design for this chisel is intended to reduce this hand-to-cutting-edge distance. The short blade means that the wrist movement is more direct and less exaggerated. The handle, hooped at the crown, resists heavy mallet use. The longer, tapered shape of the handle also makes it comfortable to use.

This is not the perfect chisel for every job. It will not cut a 2-inch (50-mm) deep mortise. There are better designs for cutting dovetails. And this chisel is not great for large paring jobs. What it excels at, however, is the other 70 percent to 80 percent of our work: notching, shallow mortising, paring tenons and dovetails, inletting, and paring small parts.

The shortness of the blade may be a matter of concern. Although it allows for better control, it may seem too short-lived to justify the amount of energy invested. It may seem that such a short chisel would last no more than a year. Mine are about five years old and are nowhere near in need of replacement. With careful sharpening and honing (but no more carefully than with any other tool), I suspect that a woodworker can use about ⅛ inch (3 mm) per year in heavy professional use.

Why then are blades normally longer? In part, because we think we consume more than we do, manufacturers feel obliged to satisfy their customers. (It is interesting to observe that Japanese chisels—quite the rage for about ten years—have much shorter blades. This condition was imposed by Japanese craftsmen and met accordingly by the manufacturers.) Additionally, manufacturers design and build for the general market, not the specific customer. Thus, the long-bladed chisel is a general-purpose tool. Like the screwdriver that never quite fits any screwhead but is handy as a pry bar, a can opener, and an ice pick, the general-purpose, long-bladed chisel fails at its primary task.

The blades of these bench chisels may also seem thick; I prefer the heft. I dislike even the thought of anything fragile or delicate about a chisel that is struck. The greater thickness also produces a larger bevel at the cutting edge which is easier to sharpen and hone.

MATERIALS

Steel: For a smaller chisel, up to ½ inch (13 mm), use ³⁄₁₆-inch (5-mm) thick stock. Old files and small leaf springs are good sources.

Ferrule: Copper or brass tubing.

Hoop: For heavy-use tools, I prefer steel pipe, though a thick-walled tubing of brass or copper would probably work as well.

Handle: Hardwood. Maple, hickory, and most fruitwoods work well, as do many exotics.

PROCEDURE

1. Anneal or normalize the steel stock.

2. Prepare the blank. Cut the stock to rough length with an abrasive cut-off wheel or a hacksaw. If you are using old file stock, remove the teeth. If you are using round or oversized stock, forge it to rough shape. You can also cut it to length using the hardy. Leave sufficient material to smooth to final shape.

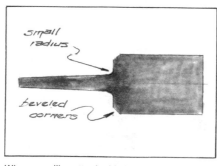

When you silhouette the blade, round the shoulders of the tang to alleviate stress cracks during hardening. The shoulders of the blade should also be rounded if they will extend beyond the diameter of the handle.

3. *Grind to shape.* The area where the blade meets the tang should be left with a slight radius on either side. Squaring that corner seems to encourage stress at that point that can result in cracking during hardening. Allow the tang to flare a little into the blade.

4. *Smooth and refine the blade.* Use progressively finer abrasives to 400-grit.

5. *Establish the hollowgrind.* Leave at least 1/16 inch (2 mm) at the cutting edge. Less thickness is very easy to burn during hardening.

6. *Harden.* Heat the blade to a light cherry red and quench in oil. Unlike a knife, the cutting edge should enter the oil first. Because oil is a slower quench, the greatest quench should go to the blade first. Use the file test to verify hardness.

7. *Clean and polish.* The backside of the blade should be smoothed to 600-grit and honed absolutely flat on the benchstone. You will find it easier to do this now, rather than after the handle is mounted.

8. *Temper.* Temper the blade from the cutting edge to the last 1/4 inch (6 mm) before the tang to straw. The last 1/4 inch (6 mm) of blade and the tang should be peacock to blue.

9. *Handle.* Turn the handle, mounting the hoop and ferrule. I usually finish the handle while it is still mounted on the lathe. Sometimes I use beeswax instead of the two coats of tung oil. If you use the wax in solid form, you can apply it directly to the handle while it is spinning on the lathe. Rub in the wax with a cloth after application. Let the handle cool for a few minutes and then buff the handle with a smooth, lint-free cloth while the lathe is turning. This coating provides a non-darkening finish that has a very nice feel to your hand. It also provides adequate protection for the wood.

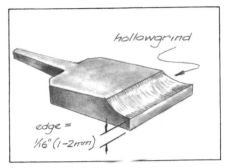

Only establish the hollowgrind. Removing more metal at that edge may result in burning the edge during hardening.

Quench the blade in oil using an up-and-down motion. Water is too harsh for the quench and a stirring motion could warp the blade with uneven cooling.

Hone the back of the blade until it is absolutely flat.

A Mortise Chisel

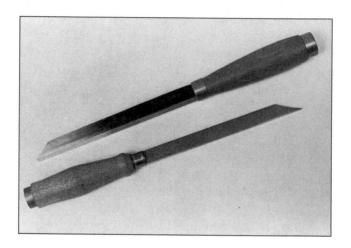

Letting in a mortise in hardwood requires a special chisel. In addition to being able to hold an edge, a mortise chisel needs to have some mass to it. It must be able to accept blow after blow from a mallet and conduct that energy directly to the cutting edge. It needs to be sharp enough at the cutting edge to properly shear the mortise ends, yet massive enough and flexible enough to withstand prying against them. And finally, the mortise chisel needs to be usable — heavy enough to do the job, yet light enough to use comfortably all day long.

DESIGN

There are mortise chisels that are more massive than this design; I have used some. My major complaint is that what these chisels provide in mass and energy, they lose in manageability. As a furnituremaker, most of the work I do requires tools that provide sensitivity and control. I like to imagine that this is expressed in the work. It's a frame of mind that is transferred from the work we do to the object we are making. The "how" of our work then has some reality in the "object" of our work. The tool needs to fit not only the physics of the task, but our sense of how we do it.

I do not like the feel of the typical mortise chisel. At 11 to 14 inches (280 to 360 mm), the chisel wants to sway when held down near the cutting edge to line up the cut. The first blows with the mallet are, therefore, tentative. Shortening the blade helps. There is less lever above your hand for gravity to deflect.

Many commercial mortise chisels thicken as they rise into the handle. The intent is, I presume, to strengthen that area of the chisel and to add to its mass. It is unlikely that a furnituremaker is ever going to stress a blade sufficiently to merit such reinforcement. A blade that is roughly square in cross section and properly tempered provides more than adequate strength. (The exception, of course, would be chisel sizes of ¼ inch (6 mm) or less. In these smaller sizes, additional thickness *is* necessary.)

Any chisel that is struck regularly with a mallet ought to be double-hooped: a ferrule at the tang end of the handle and a hoop at the mallet end. Because mortise chisels are struck a bit harder, I use copper tubing for the smaller chisels and steel pipe for the larger sizes. Most commercial chisels have a light-gauge metal ring that is so thin it is dimpled to remain on the handle. These rings do little to prevent the handle from splitting at the ferrule or mushrooming at the butt.

Because the handle is put to such punishment, it needs to be made of a tough wood. I like elm, hickory, and oak, in that order. Elm rives, or splits, very poorly (which is good). Hickory, though a bit too resilient, makes up for it in hardness and toughness. Oak is a third choice. It is becoming difficult to find nice, tight-ringed oak. Many exotics meet or exceed these three domestics. (Balua, keruing, apitong, and merbau can sometimes be found as crating material from the Orient and make excellent handles.)

MATERIALS

Steel: For smaller chisels of ¼ inch (6 mm) or less, flat stock (jointer, planer, or saw blades; rotary mower blades; leaf springs) is easier to deal with. For larger chisels, automobile coil springs are easier to forge than shape.

Ferrule: Copper tubing on chisels up to ½ inch (13 mm); steel pipe on larger sizes.

Hoop: Steel pipe.

Handle: Elm, hickory, oak, many exotics.

PROCEDURE

1. Anneal the steel. Medium cherry red and slow cooling.

2. Size the stock. Leave extra material on the tang end of the stock. Whether you are forging, or merely cutting and grinding, keep the extra stock attached for use as a grip and for cooling. You will remove it before you shape the tang.

3. Shape the blade. If you are making a smaller mortise chisel, this is primarily a grinding exercise. In cross section, however, mortise chisels are relieved slightly toward the face of the chisel from the back. This is to provide clearance for all but the cutting edge of the blade. Producing this slight taper is best done with the gradualness of a file. If this is to be a larger chisel from other-than-square stock, you will have to forge the blade. Remember that forging temperature is light orange down through red. Squaring the stock is a matter of flattening one side with a hammer as the anvil flattens the other. The anvil side will always produce a slightly smaller flat; you should even the opposing flats before starting the adjacent sides. When the flats are even, rotate the stock 90 degrees and flat-

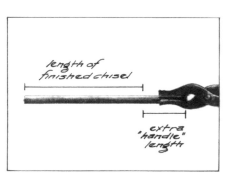

Allow some extra room at the end of the blank for the convenience of handling it during forging.

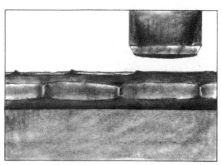

Squaring round stock for the blade requires care. Overlap the hammermarks so that the sides flatten evenly.

ten the stock to the same degree as the first two flats. Keeping the progress even is important. With each blow, the stock is elongated and thinned. If one side develops irregularities, the correction is to flatten it. As you flatten, the stock becomes thinner. At some point you will lose the thickness that you need. (For the same reasons, it is a good idea to start out with round stock that is at least 3/16 inch (5 mm) larger than the dimension you are working toward.) If it takes ten or twelve heats to obtain squareness, that is okay. There is no competition here—only you, the forge, and your steel.

4. Shape the tang. Now you should trim the blank to length. For smaller chisels in flat stock, shaping the tang is either a sawing exercise or a heavy grinding job. Leave the junction between the tang and the shoulder of the blade rounded. Sometimes during hardening, stress cracks will develop here—especially if the material is nicely squared. Wait until after tempering to square it up.

If you are forging your blade, you need to cut to length as well. Figure the exact length you will need, and subtract ½ inch (13 mm). The tang will grow at least that much as you shape it. Make the tang square in cross section, just as the blade is. Start the taper at the end of the tang with angled hammerblows. Hold the steel at an angle to the face of the anvil. Rotate hammerblows to each flat frequently, particularly as the tang thins. Try to establish a rhythm as you work. One blow, two blows, rotate to second side. One blow, two blows, rotate to third side. One blow, two blows, rotate to fourth side . . . and so on. You need not be musical. Once you have the rhythm, you will develop tempo. It should be fun. Try to relax with it. Check regularly for alignment. Tangs seem to wander and drift off-center. Be alert. Also watch the heat of the tang. As it thins, it will heat much more rapidly than the blade. It is very easy to burn. If you see those telltale white sparks bursting at the tip of the

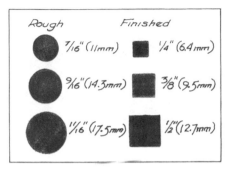

When you square round stock at the forge, the steel will elongate and diminish in thickness. Use this chart as a rough gauge of where to start.

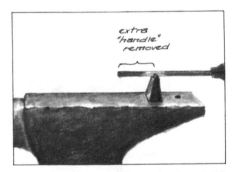

Use the hardy to remove the extra handle material. Remember to square and bevel the hardy cut at the grinder.

To forge the taper of the tang, elevate the blade from the anvil and angle the hammerblows.

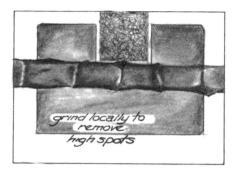

Use the grinder to flatten the cusps of the hammerwork.

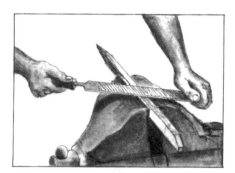

Drawfiling the flats of the chisel is an accurate method of trueing the blade.

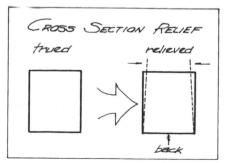

The correct shape for the blade is with the top slightly smaller than the back. This is necessary for clearance when cutting mortises.

tang, cut off the burned portion. Burned steel is not even usable on the tang of the tool. Once the forging is done, take the steel to a medium red and allow it to cool slowly.

5. ***Refine and smooth the shape.*** If you are working flat stock, you have only a little smoothing and polishing. You want the back of the chisel to be absolutely flat and smooth. I usually polish to about 400-grit before heat treatment; it is easier to clean afterward.

If you have forged a blade, you probably have at least some file work. If there are major irregularities on the flats, you may want to use the grinder. Be cautious. It is very easy to focus too intently on a relatively minor blemish when grinding and turn it into a major problem. Work lightly. Localize the grinding. With the major bumps gone, you can focus on filing. Using long, even strokes that are at a diagonal to the long axis of the blade and working the entire length will flatten all but the most distorted blades.

After the sides have been flattened, relieve the sides of the chisel from the back to the top. $\frac{1}{32}$ inch (1 mm) is sufficient relief on either side. It is easier to square first, even though you will be sloping the sides inward toward the face. Squaring the whole blade not only gives a better reference, but should there be some irremovable irregularities in what was to become the back of the chisel, you may simply rotate and redesignate. I use the grinder to shape the tang. The offset at the shoulder of the blade as it comes down to the tang ought to be approximately $\frac{1}{8}$ inch (3 mm). The stone will leave a naturally rounded corner, which you should leave rounded. A little evening of the shoulders is usually required. It is difficult to line up all four edges using the grinder. Refine them carefully with a file. These will be the stops that prevent the blade from driving through the handle. They ought to meet the handle uniformly flush. When the tang is finished, smooth the blade to 400-grit.

6. *Establish the hollowgrind.* Be sure to leave at least ¹⁄₁₆-inch (2-mm) thickness at the cutting edge. For those who have forged blades: Yes, you could have rough-shaped the bevel for the hollowgrind when you were at the forge and saved time at the grinder. But it takes practice. It is very easy to distort the end. I usually "upset" the end first to gather a little extra thickness before attempting to set the bevel, and this requires a little more skill. If you would like to try, go back to the forging step. You have "flattened" the sides of the blade but not yet started shaping the tang. First of all, inspect the end that will become the bevel. Look for the slightest hint of a fold, and grind the fold away. At the grinder, grind a slight bevel on all four edges. Heat only 1 inch (25 mm) of the end to a light orange and, holding the blade vertically to the face of the anvil with the cool end up, use the hammer to tap the cool end. This will cause the hot end, which is square to the anvil, to gradually thicken or swell. Ideally, it will swell evenly. In reality, it will more likely want to bend or distort to one side. Corrections are made down at the base by tapping against the bevel while holding the blade at an angle to the anvil face. Controlled blows are more important than force; begin by tapping rather than swinging. Not much of a swell is required; ¹⁄₁₆ inch (2 mm) will suffice. Now, when you bevel one side of the chisel and then correct the sides for the subsequent bulging, the blade will come back to full width rather than a taper.

7. *Harden the blade.* Light cherry red is the color of heat. If any dimension of the blade is ³⁄₁₆ inch (5 mm) or less (excluding the tang), use an oil quench. Thin blades should enter the quench as knives would: edgewise. Blades that are ³⁄₁₆ inch (5 mm) and larger will usually withstand a brine bath. There are never guarantees in blacksmithing, but the extra hardness and depth of case resulting from a brine quench are worth the slight risk, particularly in a larger tool. Chisels should enter the

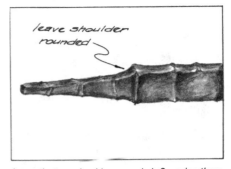
Leave the tang shoulders rounded. Squaring them may set up stress cracks during hardening.

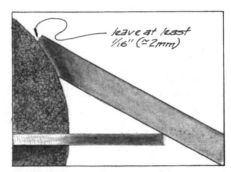
The edge should be blunt to reduce the chances of the cutting edge burning during hardening.

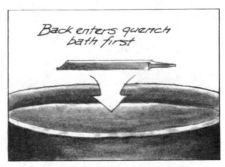
Mortise chisels of a ¼ inch (6 mm) or more will take a brine quench. Narrower chisels should be quenched in oil. The back should enter first since it is more critical that the back be fully hardened.

brine bath with the bevel up and back down, the long axis of the blade parallel to the surface of the bath. Do not hesitate to quench, but at the same time do not splash. The quench ought to be a ginger movement; the steel needs to escape that vapor envelope.

8. *Clean and polish the blade.* Remember that it is brittle and fragile at this stage.

9. *Temper.* If this is a narrow chisel, treat it as you would a knife. Apply the heat to the face or top of the chisel and let the color run to the back of what will become the cutting edge. Temper the top to vermilion-peacock, but keep the back to a medium straw color. The last 1 to 1½ inches (25 to 40 mm) of blade before the tang and all of the tang ought to be blue. Heavier chisels are difficult to temper this way. The steel heats and colors from one side to the other very quickly. As a matter of practice, I usually leave the cutting edge and first 2 inches (50 mm) of the blade a medium straw and let the lovely spectrum spread through brown, to vermilion, to peacock, to purple, and finally to blue. I run the last 2 inches (50 mm) of the blade and the whole tang blue. (Though this may seem extravagant—allowing only 2 inches (50 mm) of hard cutting blade—I have yet to use up my first blade. And the gradation of colors is not only beautiful, but I believe that the tempering it indicates makes for a strong blade.)

10. *Handle the chisel.* Handle-ing is done as described for the screwdriver in Chapter 4. For chisels up to about ⅜ inch (10 mm) the necked-down ferrule should provide adequate resistance for the blade's shoulders. On larger chisels—especially if you intend to use them for framing or rough work—seat a steel washer at the base of the shoulders. Simply lock an appropriate size washer in the vise and square out the hole to fit your tang. The shoulders should sit flush on the washer all the way around. After seating the blade, fair down the washer to the diameter of the handle.

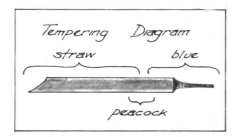

Apply the tempering heat to the tang end of the chisel first, gradually reducing the heat toward the cutting edge. Most of the tool should be straw.

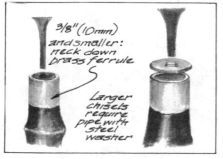

Since mortise chisels receive some heavy mallet blows, additional refinements at the handle will extend the tool's life.

11. Hone the edge. No discussion of a mortise chisel seems to pass without some comment on the type of edge it should have. Some colleagues insist on a hollowgrind on everything, including mortise chisels. Others say that it should be a flat grind. The British seem to favor a convex grind. I personally use the hollowgrind on mortise chisels unless I know that I will be using them for framework or other really heavy work. Then I admit to using a flat grind with a secondary bevel. If I chip the point regularly, even with the second bevel, I steepen the angle. This is not a purist's approach. It's just too much work to keep a convex angle well maintained.

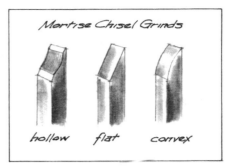

Every craftsman has his own preference for the chisel's bevel.

A Dovetail Chisel

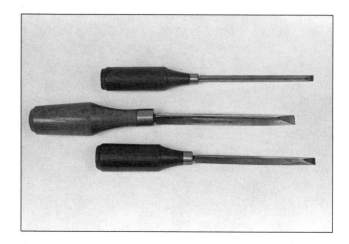

Cutting dovetails by hand is one of those details of the craft that (done with restraint and balance) rightly bespeaks skill and mastery. While it is not the most difficult of joints to cut by hand, it can be one of the most elegant. Done with an artful eye and technical excellence, the dovetail can actually "make" a piece of furniture. The work becomes "that chest with those dovetails" instead of "you know . . . that big box in the living room."

Almost every woodworker has his or her own technique for the dovetail: scribe boards to hold the line straight and the chisel vertical, clamps and clamping boards to hold certain angles or positions for sawing. There are elegant-looking gauges for marking and layout work.

My own oblation has been the dovetail chisel. Admittedly, this is not a tool that I use every time I cut dovetails. For run-of-the-mill drawer stock and shop-grade work, I usually use a butt chisel. But for those cases that show, for those times when there is only one chance for a good run of dovetails, I use

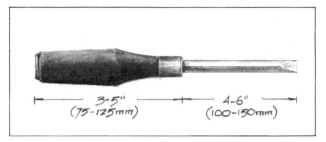

The dimensions of the Dovetail Chisel. For cutting dovetails by hand, no tool is more easily maneuvered than the dovetail chisel. It will not pinch the corners of the tails.

the dovetail chisels. It isn't that these chisels would not work for everyday tasks, it's that using them means using another chisel as well. For wider pins and tails, these chisels are too narrow to make the stop-cut in one or two passes.

DESIGN

The obvious advantage to this tool is that the inside corners of the tails are not pinched by the edge of the chisel. For truly delicate dovetails, such as on small jewelry boxes or small drawers, this is a significant advantage. When the point of a dovetail is barely more than a saw kerf wide and the flare is to only $3/16$ inch (5 mm), these chisels are a delight to work.

MATERIALS

Steel: Taper or cantsaw files of appropriate dimensions. (Forging this triangular shape would be difficult. If you were planning on producing a number of these chisels, you could make a *swage*—a stamp for shaping metal with a hammer—and swage the cross section to the triangular shape. For limited production, using the available shape makes more sense.)

Ferrule: Brass or copper tubing. (I do not hoop these handles. The delicate nature of the

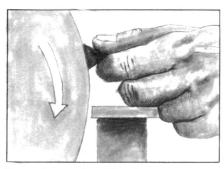

Use a delicate touch and the grinder to remove the file teeth. Most problems at the grinder are a matter of too much pressure and too little control. Quench the steel frequently.

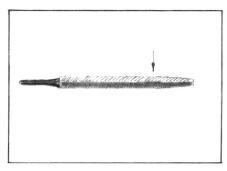

Tapers or three-cornered files make excellent blanks for dovetail chisels. The taper of the file, however, needs to be removed to produce a consistent cross section.

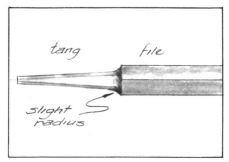

The tang shoulders should be slightly rounded to reduce the chances of cracking during hardening.

work done with these tools does not require a hoop.)

Handle: I usually keep some exotic scraps for a tool this specialized. Rosewood and ebony are particularly extravagant. Because the work these chisels do never requires a heavy mallet blow, I use exotics that may be too brittle for a heavy service handle.

PROCEDURE

1. Select steel stock. In selecting the stock, consider that the steel will be reduced about $1/16$ inch (2 mm) when you remove the file teeth and smooth the surfaces.

2. Anneal. Heat to medium cherry red and cool slowly.

3. Remove the file teeth. I prefer to use a grinder for this work. File teeth always seem to load up with firescale. After grinding, file smooth. If this is a taper file, the last one-quarter to one-third of the file is gradually reduced (hence the name "taper"). I prefer my blades to be even the length of the chisel, so I remove this tapered portion with a hacksaw.

4. Establish the hollowgrind. This is probably the most difficult of the procedures. The face of a dovetail chisel is a ridge. It does not lie flat or make good contact with the grinder's worktable. With a little practice and a light touch you can probably set up your hollowgrind and make it even. It is easier to cut a V-notch in a small piece of wood and use it as an auxilliary rest. The face of the blade rests in the notch, and the block mates evenly with the worktable. Hang the block by the grinder and use it again when you finish the hollowgrind and later, when you need to resharpen.

5. Refine the tang. A file's tang is often less than precise. Clean and square it with a file. You want all three edges to meet evenly at the handle. Leave the junction of tang to blade a little rounded. It reduces the chances of cracking during hardening.

6. *Smooth to 400-grit.*

7. *Harden the blade.* Be cautious of overheating. The edges as well as the tang are susceptible to burning. If it is a very fine blade, use your torch. Even the propane torch will bring the smaller sizes to color. If the chisel is ¼ inch (6 mm) or less, use an oil quench. The back of the chisel enters first.

8. *Smooth and polish.* Use a backup board during buffing. These tools are very brittle in their fully hardened condition. I have snapped a few during buffing from nothing more distressing than vibration. A small groove in the backup board seems to stabilize the whole operation.

9. *Temper.* Heat the bottom one-third to straw. On the top two-thirds of the blade, let the color run slowly to blue, including the tang. This is sometimes difficult to do in the smaller sizes. The edges color very quickly; the center requires more heat. When the color does move to the center, it moves quickly. The only solution is to build heat slowly.

10. *Handle the chisel.*

11. *Finish the hollowgrind and hone.*

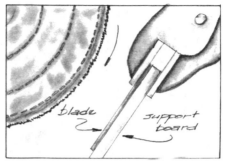

For small or delicate parts that require buffing, use a hardwood board to support the work. It is not only more effective but it is also much safer.

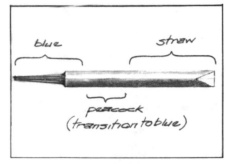

The dovetail chisel is tempered like most other chisels, and should be heated from the tang end first.

6

Carving Tools

A Fishtail Gouge

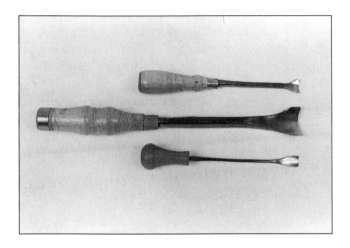

The gouge is generally considered a carver's tool. As the shape of its cutting edge suggests, it is used to cut a channel in wood. This is an oversimplification; the gouge is typically a hollowing tool. Depending on the sweep, it may be used to define a gentle hollow or an abrupt depression. But the gouge can be used for rounding as well. Inverted, the cutting edge of the gouge will refine an exterior radius. Done with care, this use can produce an edge treatment that has a warmth and character not possible with a shaper or router. The gouge is also efficient at heavy stock removal. I used to use a heavy auto-body grinder for hollowing chair seats. It was a noisy and very dusty process. A large gouge and heavy mallet have proved to be faster and also much tidier.

Most gouges manufactured today reflect their method of manufacture. Dropforging produces a clean, relatively blemish-free blank that is then ground, heat-treated, and polished in not much more than the twinkling of an eye. These are primarily full channel gouges: gouges that have a constant-sized channel for most of the blade length. While this style has proved to be handy to most carvers over the past century or so, it was probably not the original design for a gouge.

The cutting head of the fishtail gouge is a fan shape that narrows into the shaft. The channel is therefore of a diminishing width, and the profile of the edge changes in its curve. Consequently, as the gouge is sharpened and the cutting edge moves up the blade, the profile changes. This is probably the only drawback to the design. If your carving requires a ⅝ inch (16 mm) No. 9 gouge, this could be a serious drawback. If you are the type of carver who approximates the need to suit the developing situation, this is not a problem.

There are certain advantages to the fishtail design: maneuverability and quality of cut. The fishtail, being smaller overall than the full channel gouge, can get into hard-to-reach areas. When combined with a bend in the shaft, it can do some remarkable acrobatics. And, as Alex Weygers points out in his book *The Making of Tools*, the conical channel of a fishtail, when properly sharpened, provides for the severing of wood fibers at the outer edges of the gouge first. This results in little or no tear-out when cutting across the grain. This is not only useful in traditional carving, but it is particularly useful in hollowing chair seats as well. If most of the shaping is done cross grain with a large fishtail, the result requires relatively little smoothing.

DESIGN

Gouges are sized by width and sweep. Width designation is in inches or millimeters. Sweep is a designation assigned to a particular curve and usually runs from 1 through 9, shallowest to deepest. These are manufacturer's designations. As you are

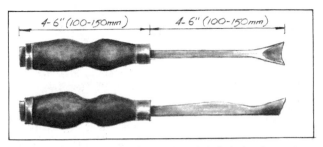

The dimensions of the Fishtail Gouge. Not strictly limited to the province of woodcarvers, the fishtail gouge is also handy to woodworkers for shaping irregular or small parts.

making gouges for your own use and not for nationwide distribution, you need not necessarily observe them. Slight, medium, and deep sweeps, in widths of ½ inch (13 mm), ⅝ inch (16 mm), and 1¼ inches (30 mm) respectively, represent a relatively complete carving set. These nine gouges would suit most of the needs of a furnituremaker and would probably be an excellent starter set for a carver.

The shaft of the tool is thicker in height than in width. This lends strength to the primary load direction of the tool, and more importantly, it provides for a comfortable hold. A slight cranking at the neck of the tool allows for clearance.

The shape of the handle is a matter of personal taste. There are probably twenty basic shapes and several variations on each of them. I have come to prefer the bolder "double bump" on large tools; I use these tools on chair seats with a heavy mallet and I like the positive grip. Smaller tools are different. When using a smaller gouge I seldom use a mallet. One hand is on the shaft of the tool guiding it; the other hand is on the handle providing the motion. For this sort of tool I prefer a relatively flat-sided handle. It allows me to put my shoulder or chest to the work. For very small tools I like a palm-style grip. By flexing the hand, you can generate a short, solid stroke that is easy to control.

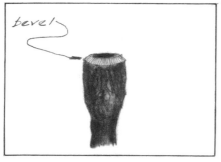

To avoid folding the steel over itself, bevel the upset head at the grinder.

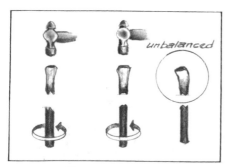

Upsetting steel is a relatively slow process that requires patience and attention. Avoid heavy blows. They will invariably lead to an unbalanced thickening of the blank.

MATERIALS

Steel: Automobile and truck coil springs are excellent for this project. The round format is easier to deal with than any angular stock would be. They are also cheap . . . occasionally free. Use the larger diameter springs for larger tools. Even small garage door springs are useful for small, delicate tools.

Handle: As smaller gouges are not struck, most any hardwood is satisfactory. (I prefer heavier woods for balance.) Handles for larger tools should be a tough hardwood: elm, hickory, or oak.

Ferrule: In addition to the many suitable pieces of ferrule material that accumulate in a shop over time (copper, brass, steel—even aluminum—tubing, as well as plumbing caps, hydraulic fittings, and cartridges), ferrules can be made by hard-soldering a band into a tube.

Hoops: Hoops for chisels ought to be tough. Steel tubing and pipe are good choices.

PROCEDURE

1. Section the blank. Use an abrasive cut-off wheel, forge and hardy, or a hacksaw. On smaller tools, leave a little extra material for a grip.

2. Upset the head. If this tool is to have a cutting head that is going to be larger than the diameter of the stock will produce during forging, you will need to upset the material at the one end of the stock. First grind the end of the blank flat and smooth. You want it square to the sides. Next grind a slight bevel around that edge (smaller bevels for small tools, larger bevels for large tools). Heat ¾ to 1½ inches (19 to 40 mm) of the end to a light orange. From the forge to the brine, quickly quench ⅛ inch (3 mm) of the now glowing tip. This will help prevent folding and distortion at the end of the upset. If this is a small diameter stock, hold the cold end down to the anvil and with a straight, controllable hammer, tap down against the heated steel. Rotate the blank as you do so; this will help to even the blows. If this is heavier stock—¼ inch (6 mm) or larger—it is usually easier to work the cold end with the hammer while holding the heated end against the anvil. In both cases, try to keep the blank as perpendicular as possible. Use the last bit of each heat to correct any distortions. Also try re-establishing the bevel as well as evening any irregular bulging that may appear.

The first time I tried upsetting, it took about ten heats. For some it may only require five heats. Be patient. The work is actually being done even though it may not be apparent. When you finish, regrind the bevel on the edge of the upset.

3. Forge the shaft. If the stock did not require upsetting, this is the first step. You need a clear picture in your mind of exactly how you want this tool to look. Look at the blank. So much needs to be cutting head and neck. The shaft needs to be so long. The tang should be about one-third the length of the shaft. With the picture clear in your mind, begin to flatten the shaft of the tool. Shape it perpendicular to the cutting edge. Because you do not want the shaft to move in any particular direction, use the flat face of the hammer to flatten the shaft. Overlap hammerblows to make the shaft sides as smooth as possible. The shaft should be about twice its width in height. This will provide a good hand hold during use. When working the neck area of the tool, let the cutting head bend in either direction as you let the shaft swell into what will be the cutting head. Be certain to even your strokes from side to side. You are striving for perfect symmetry. Flatten past where you envision the tang's shoulders, but do not thin this area any more than you did the shaft.

4. Forge the head. With the shaft and shoulders

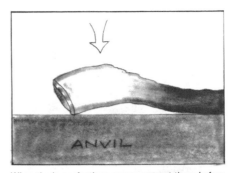

When the imperfections occur, correct them before they are too large to correct. Simply straightening this bulge will not correct the head.

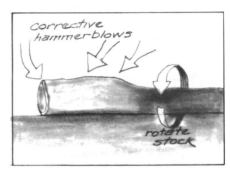

Corrective hammerblows may correct this bulge. The smith would be more likely to correct it at the grinder, however.

The head of the gouge is left unsupported while you forge the shaft to shape.

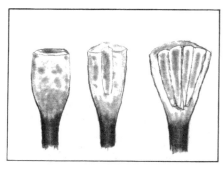

The cross peen hammer is used to fan the upset head to shape. Accuracy is more important than power.

established, begin shaping the cutting head; it should be forged at 90 degrees to the ridge of the shaft. Heat the head to light orange. Again, with a clear picture of the shape in your mind, flatten the cutting head. If this is to be a wide fan shape, use the cross peen hammer and peen parallel to the long axis of the head. If you envision somewhat less widening of the fan, use the flat face of the hammer; it spreads the steel evenly in all directions. If you want a longer, less pronounced fan, use the cross peen perpendicular to the long axis of the cutting head; it will lengthen the fan without widening it much. More flattening should be done near the cutting edge. Let the cutting head thicken and narrow as it approaches the neck and shaft of the tool. You will want more heft here. Do not flatten any area to less than 1/16 inch (2 mm). In fact, you want to leave this area somewhat thicker than its final size, since forging the channel of the gouge will reduce the thickness.

Keep that image of the tool clearly in your mind. At the same time, try to relate it to where you are in the process. Not all of forging is hammerwork and maintaining a fire; if you watch a professional smith at the forge, notice how often he or she will inspect the work. Inspect your progress and diagnose any errors, or catch the imperfections before they become errors, and forge on. Most of metalwork is like woodwork in that you need to know when to stop.

With the fan shape established, you need to set the channel in the gouge. This will require working the steel against another piece of steel with the appropriate curve. The anvil's horn is one such piece of steel. For most large- and medium-sized gouges, the horn of the anvil will produce the correct curve somewhere on its surface. (The horn is intentionally not a regular-sided cone.) For smaller gouges and for particularly deep gouges, you will need to find your own appliances. I have used pipe

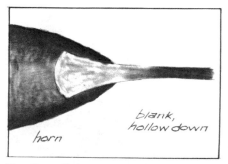

blank, hollow down

horn

Since the anvil's horn is not symmetric, it offers a variety of shapes for forming the sweep of the gouge. Other shapes can be found in the scrap pile and locked into the leg vise for the same purpose.

(threads removed), steel rod, even a section of old auto camshaft. Anything that you can secure in the vise that is iron or steel will probably work as a swage.

Heat the head to light orange and center the head with long axes parallel, on the swage. This is controlled work, not heavy forging. Use the flat face of the hammer to set the shape and center of the channel. The blows should be firm but controlled. The shaft of the tool should be somewhat elevated: 3 to 5 degrees. You want only part of the swage to shape the channel. The heavier shaping (deeper part of the channel) is toward the cutting edge and nearly full-depth at the cutting edge. The channel should narrow toward the neck and disappear before it reaches the neck. This is the outline of the cone channel. Check for alignment of the tang to cutting edge; correct as necessary. If the cutting head is tilted, heat to light orange. Use a light touch with the vise and correct any surface irregularities with the hammer. Finalizing the channel later will be much easier and more permanent if everything is true now. After aligning, twisting and hammering to correct, heat the head to light orange, being careful not to overheat that thin edge. Use an appropriately small hammer to finish shaping the channel. You want the edges even and symmetrical. You may want to deepen the shape or even flatten it out somewhat. What you are after is a cone shape: deeper and wider at the cutting edge, and diminishing gradually as it approaches the neck. To avoid distorting the basic shape of the channel, be sure to back up each blow with the anvil. If necessary, go back to the swage to work out the evenness. As you work you will develop your own technique. Some prefer a concave surface to work against, such as a piece of pipe slit lengthwise. Others like to work against the swage for most of the shaping. Most beginners work better if they are able to see what they are shaping. Be as

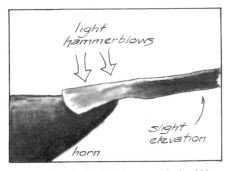

As this will be the back of the gouge, it should be as smooth as possible. Light, overlapping hammerwork here, much like planishing, will save time at the grinder and with the files.

delicate as you can in the hammerwork. You will have to smooth and even this channel eventually. A little care now will reduce the work at the grinder later.

5. *Anneal the blank.* Medium red heat cooled slowly in the dying embers.

6. *Refine the cutting head, shaft, and tang.* The cutting head will require an abrasive material that is of the same shape as the channel. Small grinding wheels that can be chucked into a drill press, on a work arbor, or in a small die grinder are all possibilities. Although it is easier to smooth out this channel with a wheel of the major diameter of your cone, a smaller wheel can be used. The most difficult part of the smoothing is to not linger in one spot for too long. Refine and smooth the channel; if you can bring it to a polish, so much the better.

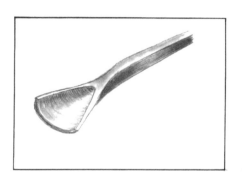

Smoothing the gouge's sweep can be done using small grinding wheels chucked in the drill press or with a die grinder. If neither is available, the file—that old standby—can do an excellent job.

I smooth the back of a gouge with a file. Though slower than some other methods, it is much easier to control the evenness of the blade's cross section. This will have to be polished, up to and including a small portion of the neck.

The shaft of the tool may be left as it emerged from the forge. You need to remove any firescale, but the shape, if you were careful and lucky, may need no further refinement. The naturally rough surface of the forging will provide a good gripping surface. If the sides are too irregular for your taste, smooth and polish them. The tool will be easier to temper with a polished surface.

The shoulders of the tang now need to be established. On a large gouge it is possible to use the hacksaw; on smaller tools, use the grinder. Do not grind or cut to the final edge of the shoulder. Leave a little extra so that you can file to the final line. The file is much more accurate, or at least, more predictable. Those shoulders need to be exactly in line with one another and perpendicular to the tang and shaft. Leave the union between the tang and

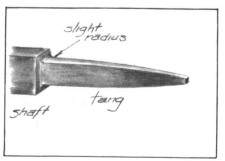

Leave the shoulders of the tang rounded to avoid stress cracks during hardening.

the shoulders slightly rounded. If there is sufficient material at the tang end, reduce, square, and taper the tang. If the shaft, the shoulders, and the tang are all the same dimension across their width (a likely occurrence on smaller tools), do not fair down the width of the tang. At the point where it joins the shoulder it should be square in section and at least as thick as the slightest part of the shaft. If there is room to fair down, then do so. Keep the work in line with the shoulders. This will provide more resistance against driving the tool into the handle during use. Although this additional shoulder area is of less importance in smaller tools, larger tools that are struck work and wear better with the added resistance. For very large gouges I even add a washer during handle-ing (see mortise chisels in Chapter 5). After I have established the shoulders, I usually do the taper work on the tang at the forge just before I harden. You may also want to either grind or file the tang to final shape.

7. Harden. Apply the heat slowly; there are a variety of thicknesses here, and you don't want to risk burning the cutting edge. Quench the blade first in an oil bath. Use vigorous figure eights. On very large gouges, 2 inches (50 mm) or more at the width of the fan, you may need to use brine for a quench. (The problem with an oil quench is that the mass of the shaft cannot be cooled quickly enough, so the heat returns and softens the head.) Check for alignment after quenching. If there is distortion that will affect the tool, reheat, correct, and reharden. Check hardness with a sharp file.

8. Smooth and polish. I use flap wheels to remove the firescale and to do light polishing on these tools. Begin with 320-grit and finish with 600-grit. As with a buffer, work below the equator of the wheel. If you do not have flap wheels, use abrasive paper and a piece of wood that is shaped appropriately. Buff the cutting head and all areas

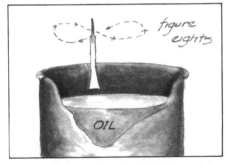

Since the gouge is thinner than ⅛ inch, use oil to quench the steel. A figure-eight motion is used because it breaks the vapor envelope that forms around the head better than an up-and-down motion would.

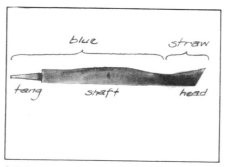

Only the head of the gouge is straw. The softer blue provides the necessary spring and shock absorption necessary for the shaft and tang.

that have been polished. You may want to leave the shaft "natural," just as it came from the forge, sans firescale.

9. Temper. Heat the cutting head to a medium straw color that darkens to a peacock at the neck and is purple to blue through the tang. Using the propane torch with a fan spreader tip, work the tang down the shaft to the neck. Keep the flame moving steadily; do not hesitate or linger anywhere. Watch the polished portion of the neck for the first signs of color. If yours is a natural finish shaft, you will not see the color until it emerges here. Let the color go no further than bronze at the neck and ideally, stop it at straw. Let the tool cool for a moment. If you were cautious in heating, beneath the rough surface of the shaft it will already be purple or blue. Now, gradually heat the neck and blade. Have a quench handy. The thicker neck will hold heat and almost flush it into the thinner blade section, down to the cutting edge. Medium straw is the color you are after. Bronze is as dark as is acceptable. Any softer and most of your time will be spent at the benchstone, putting a new edge on this tool.

10. Establish the cutting edge. On smaller gouges, ½ inch (13 mm) and smaller, a hollowgrind is difficult to establish and maintain. For this reason I use a flat or straight grind. To establish this flat grind I use a belt sander.

Hold the tool perpendicular to the belt, the long axis of the tool dipped from the handle to the cutting edge about 25 to 30 degrees. This is the cutting angle that you will establish. Hold the blank perpendicular to the direction of the belt movement. If you think of the four quadrants described by the axis of the belt and the axis of the tool, tilt the handle against the belt direction to the midpoint of that quadrant. What you are after is about a 45-degree angle to the belt direction with the cutting edge facing away from the belt's direction of movement. I always bother with the "quadrants" explanation. It is important from a safety stand-point to have the cutting edge "downstream" to avoid catching it, or the corners of the gouge's wings, in the belt. It seems easier if you think of opposite quadrants: handle upstream, blade down-stream. Begin the abrasive cut in the middle and, rotating the blade out toward the ring, describe an arc with the tang. Turn and arc to the other half of the cutting edge. Raise the whisker on the inside of the blade so that you can feel it. The turning and arcing you did should leave the cutting wings slightly forward of the center of the edge. Sharpen and hone the edge with slipstones as you would any other gouge.

11. Handle the gouge. Handle-ing is done as with any tanged tool. Drill pilot holes in the handle, heat the tang and burn it in. The alignment is most important. Larger tools that will be struck should have a steel washer with the hole squared to fit the tang and the outer edge rounded to fit the ferrule's radius. Larger gouges also require a hoop at the butt of the handle.

Skews, Spoonbills, and Cranked Necks

My interest in carving tools is that they are useful in furnituremaking primarily, and woodworking generally. My changes to the designs may or may not be necessary for carvers. It will depend on how you work.

In forging these tools I have developed a system that works a little like General Motors. The basic body of the tool remains the same, and what makes it a Chevy, an Olds, or a Pontiac is the shaping of the cutting head. A left skew, a right skew, a spoonbill, or a cranked-neck carver are not much different until you forge the head of the tool. Therefore, materials and procedures remain the same for all of the tools until you get to the cutting head.

DESIGN

As a furnituremaker I deal primarily with flat planes. For this reason most of my carving tools have a single bevel edge that is on the face (topside) of the tool. This can be easily changed at the grinder when you're establishing the cutting edge. Likewise, most of my designs have a cranked neck. If relief carvers find this distracting, omit the step of cranking the neck. In fact, most of these designs and many of the procedures are offered as starting points. Once you are comfortable with the techniques, your own designs will follow and your tools will be truly customized.

MATERIALS

See "Fishtail Gouge."

PROCEDURE

1. Upset the stock as necessary. Unless a wide fan is required, little upsetting is necessary. (See "Fishtail Gouge.")

2. Form the shaft and tang. (See "Fishtail Gouge.")

3. Form the cutting head. Skews and their relatives are all formed with the ridge of the shaft perpendicular to the cutting edge. With the blank held flat to the face of the anvil, ridge up, use the flat face of your hammer to flatten the head. Begin at the cutting edge and work back to what will be the neck. Try to maintain as flat a section as possible. As you work at the forge, estimate how much grinding will be necessary and the impact that has on what you are doing. The most common problem is to overwork the blade area and make it too thin.

Think through the processes. If it is to be a head with parallel sides, don't worry about the fan shape that is spreading out; you can true the sides at the grinder. Trying to forge the sides parallel usually results in the edges folding over. Once the head is

Form the cutting head after forging the shaft. This is much easier than trying to align the already formed shaft with the cutting head.

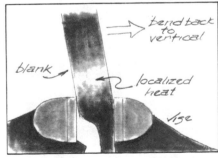
Skewing the shaft from the head will provide for clearance during use. Only a slight skew is necessary.

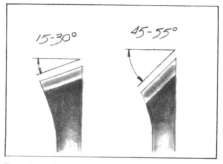

There is nothing sacred about the angles of a skew. A variety of angles can make many difficult tasks a joy.

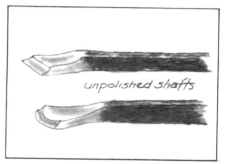

If the hammerwork is neat and clean, leave it natural. The forgework can look quite handsome and provides a better surface for gripping.

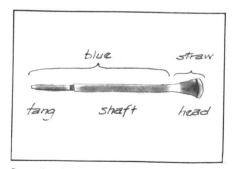

Be cautious in tempering the smaller tools. Their lighter masses will heat quickly.

flat and even, check for alignment by sighting over the face of the tool, and correct as necessary. When you check for alignment, visualize a straight line directly from tang to cutting edge, ignoring the angle of the cutting edge. You should be able to sense how it will cut. Crooks or veers, no matter how slight, deflect the energy of the hand or mallet.

To set a crank in the tool, heat the neck and head to a light orange; douse the rest of the shaft if necessary. With the tang end elevated about 10 to 15 degrees, tap the blade flat onto the anvil face. The next heat should be localized to the end of the neck and the beginning of the shaft: ½ inch (13 mm) or so into both. Lock the blade in the vise and bring it back almost parallel to the blade—almost but not quite. The deflection should be perhaps a degree or two off parallel.

4. Anneal and grind to shape. Outline the desired shape at the grinder. Skew angles are a matter of personal taste. I use a relatively severe 45 to 55 degrees for most of the work I do. Carvers I've talked to generally prefer gentler angles: 15 to 30 degrees. After shaping, establish the hollowgrind.

5. Refine and smooth to 440-grit. Although I used to spend a great deal of time smoothing and polishing the neck and shaft of my tools, I now focus only on the head. Sloth is not my reason for limiting the finishwork to the blade. Admittedly, it is quicker. More important, however, is that the unpolished shaft provides a better surface for gripping.

6. Harden and temper. Smaller tools are quite susceptible to burning. Run the forge low at first and build the heat gradually. Smaller tools will require quenching in oil. Use your judgment. Even if the tool is more than ³⁄₁₆ inch (5 mm) thick in some areas, if it changes significantly from neck to blade, use oil. Larger or thicker tools will generally tolerate a brine quench. If you are uncertain, try with oil first. If hardening is not to your satisfaction, clean the tool thoroughly, reheat, and try brine. Temper as described under "Fishtail Gouge." Thin-sectioned tools color quickly. Be vigilant.

7. *Sharpen and hone.*

8. *Handle.*

7

Knives

My first attempts at toolmaking began with knives. It was before I owned a forge and anvil and before I knew anything of metallurgy. A Sunbeam drill strapped to a bench with a thoroughly glazed 2-inch (50-mm) grinding wheel mounted in the chuck, and two very old, very dull files were the extent of my equipment. My understanding of metallurgy was limited: The color blue appearing on steel meant that the steel had been ruined in some way; car springs made good knives (a fact gleaned from Hemingway's *Old Man and the Sea*, published the year before). As I recall, the blades were made of mild steel. I was able to do a good job inletting the blade into the wooden handle—after all, I was a woodworker. (In fact, my technique for inletting partial-tang tools has not changed much since then.) The cutting edges were much too thick and blunt to cut. I probably burnished more wood with those tools than I cut. I was thirteen.

Today, I have several drawers filled with knives. While I could probably get by with four or five different knives, the luxury of being able to make my own has spoiled me. I have come to expect that distinct feeling I get from using a knife suited to its task. The curls of wood are long and even, and there is no stutter to the cut. The knife simply cuts as I guide it. No other tool offers such proximity and directness.

The knife you make for yourself is a tool, but more than a tool . . . almost an instrument. It is a knife whose handle fits your hand, whose blade suits a specific task. It is a knife that is made, not bought. More important, it is a knife made by the craftsperson who will use it. Who knows more about your hands and how they hold a knife, about the work you do, or how you want to do it?

The making of a knife is pleasant work. The metalwork is straightforward: some grinding, some heat treatment, some sharpening. The handle is no more difficult. Your first knife may take several hours to make. You will be feeling your way. Eventually, as your skills grow, you will make a knife in about an hour. As you progress, your designs will change.

There are three basic ways to make a knife: a full tang with a slab handle; a through tang with a solid handle; and a partial tang with either a slab or solid handle. The first and third of these methods are more common. The through-tang handle is used primarily to facilitate the use of animal horns and antlers as handles. Either the full-tang or partial-tang method can be used to make most any design. For this reason, I will discuss the two methods first and talk about designs afterward.

A Full-Tang Knife

A full-tang, slab-handled knife is my favorite design. Not only does the full tang lend strength to the knife, but it gives balance as well. The added weight also seems to absorb or dilute chatter. A full-tanged tool moves with more authority.

MATERIALS

Steel: Old files, jointer or planer blades, saw blades, lawn mower and edger blades, old shears, and old knife blades are all good choices. For most of my knifemaking I prefer stock that is already at the desired thickness. Forging a blade, flattening it, and grinding it to an even thickness is time consuming. A brief discussion of forging a partial tang is presented under "Partial-Tang Knives" later in this chapter.

Handles: Because knives are not struck, handle material is a matter of taste. I like the dense grain and heft of tropical hardwoods. Invariably, woodworkers have squirreled away bits and pieces of this precious stuff—sometimes to overflowing. They are cut-offs, culls, or perhaps just small sections of remarkable grain. What better use for them?

Pins: Brass or brazing rod in a variety of diameters.

Epoxy: An all purpose type.

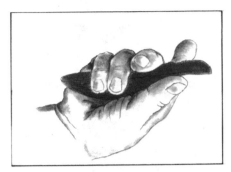

Getting the right shape is a matter of getting to know your hand and how it works.

PROCEDURE

1. Make a pattern. If this is the first time you are trying a particular design, invest some time in sketches and models. There is nothing elaborate about this work. Sketch until you think you have the idea, then cut the pattern out of masonite and test it in your hand. You usually have to make modifications, but it is time well spent. Masonite is cheap. Grinding and shaping steel only to discover that the shape does not work is the real waste.

2. Anneal the stock.

3. Transfer the pattern to the stock. How you do this depends on how you will cut the stock. If you plan to use a jeweler's saw or a hacksaw, use a machinist's scribe. The fine bright line is quite precise and easy to check. If you have access to a metal-cutting bandsaw, use a silver-colored pencil. The mark, though less precise, is easier to follow—even with the metal dust in the way. Depending on your method of cutting, be sure to leave yourself room for the kerf and the tool's "wander factor." With the jeweler's saw you can be quite precise with the marks and the kerf. The hacksaw can, at best, accomplish a quick approximation of the shape. Most of my students are better with the hacksaw than I am. The bandsaw is accurate—not so precise as the jeweler's saw, but close.

I do not recommend using the cutting torch. For small tools such as these, the torch tends to be too

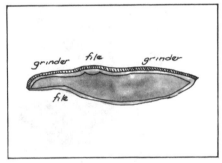

Use the grinder for outside radii and rat-tail files for inside radii.

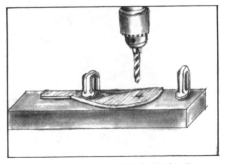

Use clamps to secure the blank for boring the pinholes.

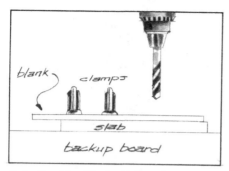

Boring the slabs of the handle is easily done using the blank as a template. Be sure to label the slabs as you bore them. Later, during glue-up, it will be less confusing.

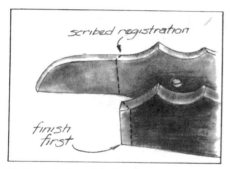

The forward edges of the handle slabs should be shaped and smoothed prior to glue-up. Once they have been mounted, it is difficult to do any shaping without scarring the blade.

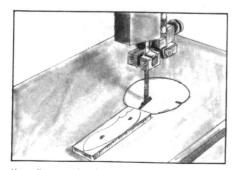

Use a jigsaw or band saw to outline the handle shapes.

coarse and can easily ruin a cutting edge. Besides, carbon steel seldom produces a clean line under the cutting head.

4. *Silhouette the tool.* Cut out the shape and refine it at the grinder. Except for some smoothing later on, this will be the final shape and size of the knife.

5. *Drill the pinholes in the tang.* Use the center-punch from your first exercise in Chapter 4 to punch the hole sites. Locate the sites ½ inch (13 mm) or so from either end of where the handle will mount to prevent splitting of the wood. Secure the blank to a backup board and secure the backup board to the drill press table. Metal, being much less forgiving than wood, has a tendency to run up on a drill bit. Even though this blank is not yet sharpened, its square corners and points can be ruthless, even at just 150 rpm. Select a drill of approximately the same size as the pins. The holes ought to be slightly larger—certainly not loose, but not anywhere near binding.

6. *Lay out handle slabs.* This is your first aesthetic choice. Which scale is attached to which side and in which direction? Scribe a line on both sides of the tang that indicates exactly how far up on the steel the slabs will be mounted. I also do the shaping and final sanding for this forward edge of the slab now, since it is more difficult to adjust one to the other after the slabs have been committed to a location by the pin holes. The insides of the slabs need to be flattened now as well. I generally smooth them with nothing finer than 100-grit. Lay one slab down as it will mate with the tang. Lay the blade over it, making certain that the forward edge of the slab is at the line you scribed for it. Use the tang as a drilling template for the slab.

Once the holes have been drilled, use a felt tip marker to identify the exact location of the tang on this slab. Although this may seem like a waste of time, I have found it to be a tremendous aid. In the frenzy of glue-up, it is sometimes easy to confuse one slab with the other. A sane person probably would not confuse them. During glue-up, especially with five-minute epoxy on a warm day, the confusion is natural.

7. Silhouette the slabs. Follow the thick felt tip line and stay about ⅛ inch (3 mm) wide of the line. When the slabs are clamped with epoxy, this extra material will serve as a trough for the squeeze-out.

8. Drill epoxy rivet holes. See "Utility Knife" in Chapter 4. Remember to centerpunch the hole sites.

9. Establish the hollowgrind. As before, do not grind a thin final edge. It would burn during hardening.

10. Smooth and polish. Don't polish the tang. Drawfile it lightly to ensure that there are no protrusions that will interfere with mounting the slabs. If the stock was rusted or pitted, clean up the tang enough so that you can view the color changes during tempering. Otherwise, the stock is probably best left a little rough. The adhesion of the epoxy will be better. Polish the blade to 440-grit.

11. Harden the knife. Heat to a light cherry red and quench in oil, cutting edge first. Unless you are doing a series of knives, using the forge for heating such a small tool is probably a waste of energy. Use the oxyacetylene torch instead. Secure the torch lightly but firmly in a vise, its flame judiciously aimed away from any conceivable combustible. This allows the use of both hands. With pliers, grasp the blank by the end of the tang and heat the spine with the torch. Heat gradually . . . just as in the forge. Keep the tool moving over the flame. Building heat too quickly in one area is a real possibility with a torch. This localized heat can conceivably warp the tool. Let the heat spread evenly and thoroughly from the spine into the cutting edge and at least half of the tang. Quench at light cherry.

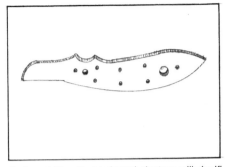

Boring additional holes through the tang will significantly increase the strength of the epoxy bond. The epoxy will form rivets that extend through the thickness of the tang and bond to the opposing slab.

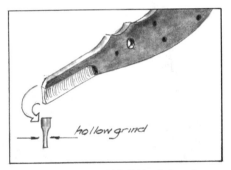

Leave the hollowgrind thick. Taking it down to a finer section would be a waste of time. If the section is too thin, it will burn off in the forge during the hardening process.

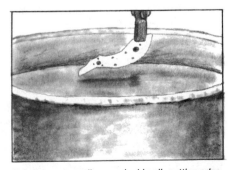

Knives are generally quenched in oil, cutting edge first. This ensures that the most important part of the knife, the cutting edge, receives the most complete hardening.

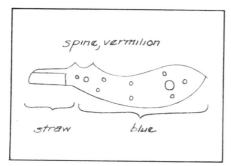

Knives generally follow the rule of a blue tang and a straw blade. Tempering the spine somewhat between these two tempers (vermilion) adds a little flex to the blade and a little rigidity to the tang.

Organizing before glue-up will save you the frustration of reaching for something that is not there while the epoxy cures on your fingertips.

Putting the pins in before glue-up helps to align the slabs. It is also less messy than pushing the pin through a hole clogged with epoxy.

12. Smooth and polish. For a knife, I usually smooth the blade surface to 600-grit and buff. The tang needs to be no brighter than 150-grit. Before you do any abrasive work, however, clean the blade thoroughly; if you don't, the quench oil and abraded material will soon clog your abrasives. After smoothing and polishing, clean all surfaces again. Highly polished surfaces are particularly receptive to the oils in your hands and will give a false reading of the temper colors if allowed to remain.

13. Temper. Tang, blue; spine, bronze to vermilion; cutting edge and most of the blade, medium straw. Go slowly. Work the spine of the blade and tang first. Watch the blade carefully. If the heat builds too quickly in the thicker spine or tang, it will run with incredible speed across the cutting edge.

14. Glue and pin the slabs. (Refer to "Utility Knife" in Chapter 4.) Before mixing any epoxy, lay out the slabs, the pins, the knife, some clamps, clean-up rags, and solvent. Be organized; know where everything is before you start the process. Do a dry fit-up using undersized pins. After glue-up, allow the epoxy to cure thoroughly.

15. Peen the pins. Use the anvil to back up each pin as it is peened. Take your time peening. The idea is to mushroom the head and a bit of the pin's shaft. Use light, controlled strokes; work the whole head of the pin. Peen the opposite side as well. The anvil will not peen; it is merely the support. Peen both heads of the first pin, then peen the second pin.

16. Shape the handle. As a woodworker, you'll have your own method. I fair the handle down to the tang at the disc sander first; it will flush the tang and slabs quickly. If the wood heats and the epoxy begins to feel soft, let it cool. It will reharden. Approach the final shaping with caution. Check the feel of the tool often. It is very easy to remove too much material. As you are shaping the handle, think about how you will use it. Get a feel for the balance of the tool. If you check often enough, you will catch that moment when it is just right.

17. *Finish the handle.* Use two coats of tung oil: The first coat is thinned about 50 percent; the second coat is thin but not diluted. Allow the finish to dry for at least one day. Buff with a clean buffing wheel. Buff gently or you will remove the finish.

18. *Sharpen and hone the cutting edge.*

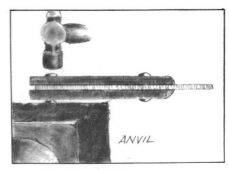

Be sure to support the opposite side of the pin or it will be driven through the handle.

A Partial-Tang Knife

While I prefer the weight and balance of the full-tang knife, the partial tang has some advantages. First of all, the design requires less steel. Even though I use scrap steel, I feel a little guilty about any waste. A partial-tang knife makes use of scraps. Small pieces of scrap steel, like the little bits of precious wood that accumulate alongside them, can be turned into useful tools.

The partial-tang format is quite compatible with forging. The full-tang knife requires a flat tang that has even sides for good adhesion to the slabs; a forged surface has to be ground flat to produce such a surface. With the partial-tang knife this surface is not so important, so you can take advantage of the benefits of forging.

MATERIALS

Steel: Same as for the full-tang knife. Allow 1½ to 2 inches (40 to 50 mm) in length and ¼ to ⅜ inch (6 to 10 mm) in width for the tang.

Handle: Same requirements as the full-tang knife.

Pin and Epoxy: This design requires only one pin.

A mock-up knife is easy to shape and modify to fit your hand.

PROCEDURE

1. Design the tool. Just as before, you need to spend some time designing the tool. I use masonite cutouts to get the feel for each knife I make. Design the tool first, then design the blade and tang configuration.

2. Anneal the steel.

3. Cut out the knife. Scribe the pattern on the steel and cut and grind to shape. The difference this time is that you need to consider the effect your forging will have. Leave sufficient material around the blade and tang to allow for clean-up at the grinder.

4. Forge the blade and tang. Because this is a thin, small forging, do not set the blank into the fire; it would be very easy to lose. Hold it with the tongs or locking pliers. Watch the color closely and heat slowly. This is delicate forgework; use a small hammer. The blows will require no more than the simple fall of the hammer to move the metal. Work the double bevel first. Use the flat of the hammer and lightly angle your blows. Hammer one bevel completely, then reverse and even the other side to match. If the blade is to taper in thickness to a point, set the taper now. Again, use gentle blows. Don't let the blank get too thin. Overworking is very easy in such small work. Don't do anything to the tang except to straighten or align it. You want as much thickness and strength here as possible. The last heat should be to anneal; just let it cool slowly.

5. Refine the shape. Establish the final shape at the grinder and smooth the blade to 400-grit. Do not hollowgrind yet.

6. Drill the pinhole in the tang. For very small knives, I have used pins that are a little under $1/16$

A wooden or stiff-paper template is an accurate method for transferring the pattern to the steel.

Forging the cutting edge requires a light touch. If it is struck too hard, the blade may be too thin to survive the hardening process.

Locate and bore the pinhole in the tang. Take care
to secure the blade with clamps when boring.

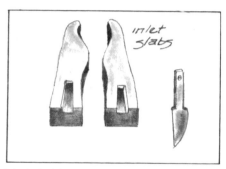

Inlet both slabs to accept the exact width and half
the thickness of the tang.

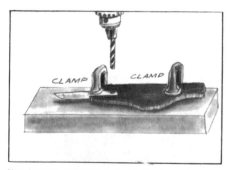

Use the tang, properly seated in its channel, as a
template for boring the pinholes.

inch (2 mm). The pinhole and pin ought to be
about a third of the width of the tang. Even on
small knives I like the hole located at least ¼ inch
(6 mm) from the end of the tang. Be sure to secure
the blank. Use a backup board and clamps during
drilling.

7. Prepare the handles. My system for handle-
ing a partial-tang knife is somewhat unorthodox.
Most knifemakers use a solid handle and bore a slot
in it. I prefer to make two halves, which I mortise
for the tang and drill for the pin. I believe this
allows for greater accuracy and thus a stronger
handle. Professional knifemakers are after the appearance that a solid block would provide. I am
after a more direct method, which is easy and still
provides a serviceable handle.

First, locate and mark the position of the tang on
each of the scales. Cut these channels with a
chisel, to a depth of half the thickness of the tang.
Test the fit of the slabs with the tang in position to
be sure that the two halves mate evenly. As with
the full-tang knife, use the tang as a template to
drill the pinholes: first in one slab and then in the
other. Be sure to secure your work.

8. Harden the tool. Unless I have a number of
these blades to harden, I use the oxyacetylene torch
for heating. With small knives, I have even used a
propane torch. Allow the heat to move from the
spine and tang into the cutting edge. Remember
how easily that cutting edge will burn.

9. Smooth, polish, and temper the steel. Because these tools are so small and brittle, use a
support board when holding them to power equipment. Buffers especially will grab and toss them
like darts. Temper the tang blue, the spine bronze,
and the rest of the blade medium straw.

10. Mount the handle slabs. While I may or may
not finish the hollowgrind on other tools at this
point, on a partial-tang knife I always wait until I
have the handle mounted. Lay out the slabs, the

knife, the pin, the epoxy, clean-up rags, solvent, and clamps. Make a dry run through the procedure.

Apply the epoxy to the first slab; be sure to coat the channel as well. Apply epoxy to the mating side of the tang. Insert the tang into the channel and push the pin into its hole, through the tang, and through the slab. Apply epoxy to the other slab, line up the pin with the hole, seat it, and squeeze. Clamp the slabs and allow the epoxy to dry.

Epoxy may not seem necessary for the proper adhesion of what amounts to nothing more than two pieces of wood. I have used modified PVA and aliphatic resin as adhesives for knife slabs, but I prefer epoxy. It seems to be more shock-absorbing and resistant. While the wood-to-wood joint has not failed using either the PVA or the resin glues, the blades have come loose in their mortises after a few years. Failures with epoxied knives are, at this point, nil.

11. Shape the handle. As with the full-tang knife, the shaping of the handle is every bit as important as the cutting edge. The handle is your means of manipulating the blade. Check its progress frequently. Hold it in your hand. Make it fit and feel right.

12. Finish the handle. Use tung oil, wax, or your favorite mixture.

13. Finish the hollowgrind, sharpen, and hone.

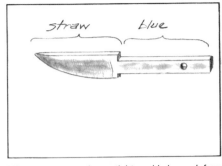

When you temper the partial-tang blade, work from the darker tang to the straw of the blade. Use a small flame and work slowly; the colors will appear and run quickly.

A Drawknife

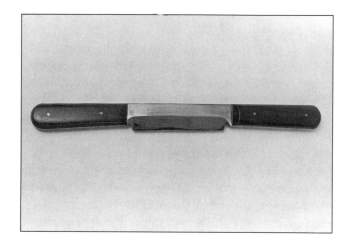

Most drawknives are not suited for furniture work. They are relatively massive tools, intended for a bolder, if not coarser, sort of work. From a purely functional standpoint, the drawknife is really nothing more than a two-handled knife whose handles oppose one another. Some blades are bent; some are straight. Some are hollow-ground on their backs. Some have handles that are offset either up or down from the blade. Some are so massive in size that they seem more suited to tapering the mast on a sailing ship than anything else. Some, usually called push knives today, are small and seem almost useful for furnituremaking or woodworking in general.

If it seems that I have not convinced myself of the value of this tool to the average woodworker, it is because I have not. A spokeshave seems to do almost the same operation but with more control. And a knife is better suited for very small work.

In the making of treen, however, the drawknife excels. Treen is an old term that refers to small kitchen objects or tools, carved toys, even small

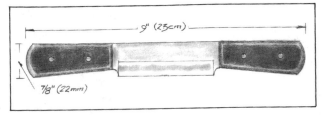

The dimensions of a pushknife. A smaller variety of the drawknife, the pushknife is intended for lighter, more controlled work.

bowls, usually made of green logs or branches. My treenware is mostly spoons, ladles, and paddles. Sometimes I work in green wood . . . mostly salvaged orchard wood, apple, plum, and apricot. The small drawknife is an excellent tool for this purpose. When roughing the treen, a drawknife will turn a shaving that is ⅛-inch (3-mm) thick or more. For such work as the back of a spoon, it can be used to leave delicate facet after facet in long, continuous rows. In fully seasoned wood, the performance is really no better than that of a spokeshave, although it seems more direct.

MATERIAL

Steel:	Worn-out files and planer blades require little work to achieve the right shape. If you choose a file, remove the teeth completely after annealing or they may set up stress in the tool during hardening.
Handles:	Dense tropical hardwoods are attractive, but most hardwoods are satisfactory.
Pins:	Metal rods of brass, copper, steel, even aluminum, are satisfactory. These handles are not very stressed during use.

PROCEDURE

1. Anneal the stock.

2. Smooth the stock. If the steel is from an old file or is rusted or pitted, now is the time to smooth and flatten it.

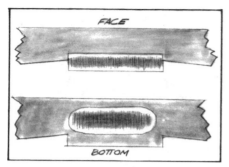

Hollowgrinding the back or bottom of the blade makes honing the tool later a much more pleasant task.

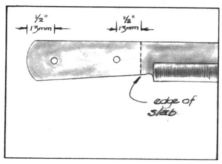

When you select the pinhole sites, locate them away from the edges of the handles. If they are too close, the handles will split.

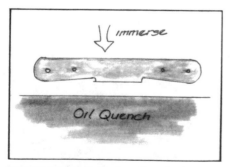

Quench the drawknife in oil, cutting edge first. The quenching motion should be vertical, up-and-down movement.

3. *Grind to shape.* The design requires little grinding. Flare the handles slightly from the edge of the blade and leave the cutting edge slightly proud of the handles. None of these elements are crucial. The hollowgrind is relatively easy to execute. Rest the spine on the grinder's tool rest and move the blade evenly back and forth. You just want to establish the hollowgrind at this point. Grind it no further than will be safe for hardening. You may want to establish a slight hollow along the back. This facilitates sharpening and honing significantly. You need a light touch along the back—a scant $1/16$ inch (2 mm) deep, at most. Polish the blade area, front and back, to 400-grit.

4. *Drill the tangs for pins.* Pins should fit the holes without binding. Remember to secure all work before drilling. Locate the holes at least $1/2$ inch (13 mm) from the ends of the slabs to minimize splitting. Since these are very small slabs, only three or four epoxy rivet holes are necessary on a tang.

5. *Prepare the slabs.* This is more confusing than with the regular knives. Pair the slabs and assign them to a particular tang. Otherwise, the preparation of the slabs is the same for the drawknife as it was for the full-tang knife.

6. *Harden the steel.* Heat to light cherry red, quench in oil—cutting edge first. Of the half-dozen drawknives that I have made, none have cracked or distorted during the quench. I have no good reason for quenching the cutting edge first, except that it worked the first time and every time since.

7. *Smooth, polish, and temper.* The blade area should be smoothed to 600-grit and buffed. The tangs can be left relatively rough as long as they are clean, exposed metal. Temper the handles blue and the spine dark bronze to vermilion. Most of the blade and the cutting edge should be a medium straw.

8. *Mount the slabs.* The procedure for mounting

the slabs is the same as mounting slabs to any full-tang knife. It is easier to complete one handle before moving to the other. Mix enough epoxy for only one side at a time. Allow both sides sufficient drying time before moving on.

9. Set the pins; shape and finish the handles. Again, refer to "Handle-ing a Full-Tang Knife" in Chapter 4 if you need to.

10. Complete the hollowgrind, sharpen, and hone. A note on sharpening: The two handles make sharpening the blade easy, but you should first check your stone's width for flatness. Although you may have tried to use the entire surface of a benchstone during sharpening, a hollow is almost always present. Using the hollowed surface of the stone will quickly ruin the straight edge that you were so careful to create, so use the edge of the stone if it is large enough.

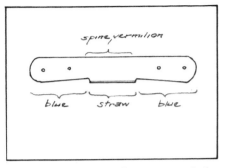

The drawknife is tempered the same as most other knives, except that it has two handles. The vermilion spine will give a little flexibility to the blade while not affecting the hardness of the cutting edge.

8

Planes

There is a distinction, and rightly so, between a tool and an instrument. Of all the tools in our shops, none is more appropriately deemed an instrument than the plane. No tool has the versatility of the plane. No tool will better prepare a surface for gluing. No tool—power or hand—can so delicately remove that merest wisp of a shaving necessary for a perfect fit. And of course, no tool will dress a piece of wood with the same depth, glow, and shimmer.

Not all planes work with such refinement, and no plane *always* works with such refinement. Planes, even good, instrument-quality planes, have their finicky side. Sometimes it seems that there is no satisfactory adjustment. Sometimes the adjustment shifts at the worst possible moment. Sometimes we think that perhaps the belt sander is a far superior tool. But more often, the well-tuned, well-fettled hand plane is a delight to use.

WOOD VS. METAL

In the tradition of all great controversies, the question of the best material for a hand plane has plagued woodworkers for generations. One side asserts, "The wooden plane moves so much more naturally over its kindred . . ." The other counters, "A metal plane has the mass and natural tendency to bear much more evenly on the planed surface than . . ." Both types have advantages and disadvantages. I own both. I have made both. A good plane is a good plane, whether it is made of metal or wood. The ultimate proof is, of course, the quality of cut. When the work has been done and the critics have come and gone, and the craftsperson too has gone, the work itself must stand or fall. The type of plane seems insignificant.

For someone trying to make a decision between planes of metal and of wood, there is no better advice than this: Try them both. Find a proponent of each side and listen to the pitch. The most important factor, however, will be how the tool feels to you. Some will prefer the mass of the metal, others the whoosh of the wood. Some will be driven to distraction adjusting a wooden plane, others will despise the gadgetry on a metal plane.

DESIGN

Functionally, all planes are the same. A blade is held rigidly at some prescribed angle within the body of the plane, and the cutting edge is adjusted in or out through the mouth of the sole. The tool needs to be held during use and so requires either a handle or a body shape to facilitate the grip.

The wedge. My approach to planemaking has been to focus on what I consider the basics and leave the finer, more ingenious touches to inventors. Even the most innovative design, incorporating grace, function, and utility, will not work if poorly executed. Yet the simplest design, if done with care, attention, and understanding, invariably exceeds expectations.

Having to adjust a plane iron with a hammer has never bothered me. (Perhaps if I had known there were other ways, it would not have been so easy.) In fact, I prefer it. There is nothing mystical to it. It is not much different from lacing and tying your shoes. How often do you overtighten the laces? With use, you will come to know your planes as well as your feet. Though the feeling is different, it is no less real.

Since I like adjusting the iron by feel, my planes are made for wedges . . . even my metal planes. The design is more flexible and requires less special tooling during fabrication. What's more, the wedge holds the blade rigidly.

The bedding angle. The bedding angle for most larger planes is 45 degrees. That is not to say that 44- or 46-degree angles would not work; they do. Nevertheless, planemakers use a 45-degree bedding angle. For some smaller planes in which the blade is mounted bevel up and there is no cap iron, the bedding angle is much slighter to facilitate curl and chip clearance.

The blade. Because you are now able to work steel, to forge it, grind it, and control its hardness, the blade should take on new interest for you. You will be able to make your own blades and cap irons. Again, however, there is nothing new or startling about the design. Concentrate on making a simple blade well. The back of the blade is flat and true. The cap iron meets the back of the blade cleanly, precisely, and without gaps. The cutting edge is clean, true, and hardened to your specifications.

The body and handle. The design of the body is a matter of taste and ergonomics. For larger planes, I prefer the traditional *horn* for the front and *collar* at the rear. But that's because I learned how to plane on that type of instrument. The lower, sleeker style of plane proffered by James Krenov has its advocates. I have seen his work and that of his students and I am impressed. The surfaces are flawless. But there is more to his work than the shape of his plane. In the smaller sizes, his lower, flatter design is easier to control. It even works well single-handedly.

But in the larger sizes I find the Krenov pattern awkward. I learned from a very precise and dogmatic teacher that the back hand pushes neither forward nor down but at precisely 45 degrees to the surface being planed. He also taught me that the forehand on the horn provides only half the pressure that the backhand does. The forehand is there to guide. Part of its job is to tilt the plane slightly at the end of the stroke and allow the backhand to rest during the recovery. This method does not work well with a design that has no formal handle.

I also prefer the more traditional style for its planes of reference. Much of what we do is done "by eye." We line up a tool with the bench, the vise, or

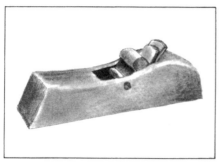

A wooden hand plane designed by J. Krenov. Notice the sleek, rounded lines that permit single-handed use.

A traditionally styled wooden hand plane. The design of this plane requires that it be used with two hands.

even another board, and cut. The human eye has a great sensitivity for this sort of referencing. What we can sense by reference is often remarkably subtle. The sides of the traditional plane are two of my references.

A Wooden Smooth Plane

There was a time, when boards were dressed and thicknessed by hand, that the term *smooth plane* referred to the last in a series of bench planes (the scrub, the jack, the jointer, and the smooth plane). This was the plane that was used to smooth that final surface. The term is still descriptive. For although the drudgery of hand-dressing stock is no longer necessary, the machines still leave their marks and the smooth plane still has its place.

Of all the many ways of working wood, I cannot think of any that is more nearly the epitome of woodworking than using a smooth plane. It is the essence of our work.

DESIGN

Planes are categorized and named by the length of their soles. The smooth plane is usually 8 to 10 inches (200 to 250 mm) long. It is compact and

easy to control. Its use presumes the trueness of
the board. Because it is short, it tracks the surface
of the board. If the board is not flat, the smooth
plane will not flatten it.

The body of the plane is rectangular in length
and roughly square in cross section. The edges and
corners are all radiused or softened to make use and
handling comfortable. A sole of dense tropical hardwood is laminated to the body. This lamination is
not a necessity, but I like the contrast. Being denser
and harder than most of the woods worked, it will
probably wear better. (I say probably because in
twenty years I have not yet worn out a sole.)

The design of the horn at the front end of the
plane should be a matter of taste and utility. Its
shape should provide a comfortable grip as well as
keep the fingers safely above the surface. I have
made and used both the straight and offset horn
patterns and I prefer the straight. I like the orientation that it provides.

The back handle, or *collar*, allows for a more even
and controlled pressure at the rear. I prefer it over a
more overt "handle-style" pattern. The rounder collar style encourages that 45-degree downward push
when using the plane.

In the throat of the plane is the heart of the

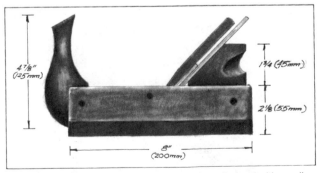

The dimensions of a smoothing plane. Properly crafted and with a well-honed blade, the smoothing plane can do some incredible work, even on figured grain.

mechanism. A freely rotating flat crossbar holds the wedge firmly against the blade and the blade against its bed. I have experimented with round crossbars, and the friction they provide is not sufficient in larger-wedge planes. The wedge itself covers all but the last ½ to 1 inch (13 to 25 mm) of the blade. I like a tough wood for the wedge, one that takes hammerblows without mushrooming. Beech and elm are good choices.

Blades for benchplane-size tools ought to be two-piece: the iron and the cap iron. While the cutting edge of the iron cuts the wood, the cap iron deflects the shaving forward. This deflection serves two purposes. First, it breaks the shaving. This frees the shaving from the wood and curls it out of the plane's throat. Without the deflection, the cut at the surface could become a rive or a split. Some wood fibers would break; the surface would not be smooth. Secondly, the cap iron lends weight and rigidity to the blade iron. Planing requires an absolutely undistorted cutting edge. The slightest movement or disturbance during the stroke is amplified by further movement and the result is chatter. Blade chatter will spoil a surface. For this reason, both the iron and cap iron need to be heavy steel at least ⅛ to 3/16 inch (3 to 5 mm) thick.

MATERIALS

Steel

Blade Iron: ⅛ to 3/16 x 1½ x 7 inches (3 to 5 x 40 x 180 mm). Saw blades and large planer blades can be worked into excellent irons.

Cap Iron: ⅛ to 3/16 x 1½ x 4 inches (3 to 5 x 40 x 100 mm).

Screw: ¼ inch x 20 flathead screw with square shoulders.

Washer: ¼ inch flat washer.

Hardwood

Full Body: 2⅜ x 2⅝ x 12 inches (60 x 66 x 300 mm). Beech and maple make good

Dimensions for the double irons.

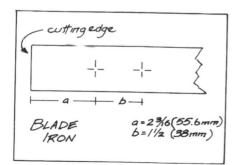

Locate the end holes for the cutting iron's slot. Clamp the work securely before boring the holes.

plane bodies and do not require a laminated sole. Most exotics, if they are properly dried, work well. If you want to laminate the side, subtract its thickness from the overall thickness of the body.

Front Horn: 2 x 2 x 7 inches (50 x 50 x 180 mm).
Rear Collar: 2 x 2 x 3 inches (50 x 50 x 80 mm).
Wedge: ⁹/₁₆ x 1½ x 6½ inches (14 x 40 x 165 mm).
Crossbar: ½ x 1 x 2½ inches (13 x 25 x 65 mm).
Pins: ⅜ inch (10 mm) dowels: two each of 2½ inches (65 mm) and of 1½ inches (40 mm).

PROCEDURE FOR THE IRONS

1. *Anneal the stock.*

2. *Cut out the blade and cap irons.* An abrasive cut-off saw works well for these 90-degree cuts. Keep everything square; nothing is as aggravating as discovering that the cutting edge is not square to *both* sides. If your stock is too wide, but only by ⅛ inch (3 mm) or so, consider enlarging the plane. There is nothing magical about the 1½-inch (40-mm) width. Simply alter your stock and cutting dimensions. If the width is simply too large, scribe a line *exactly* parallel to the opposite side. Use a hacksaw and cut wide of the line, then grind to the scribed line. Make sure both irons are exactly the same width.

3. *Cut the screw slot in the iron.* Use a centerpunch to mark a hole site that is centered in the width of the blade and 2³/₁₆ inches (55 mm) away from where the cutting edge will be. Centerpunch another hole site 1½ inches (40 mm) further up the blade. Lock the blade to a backup board and clamp it to the drill press table. Bore a ⅜-inch (10-mm) hole at each site, scribe tangent lines, and bore a series of holes between these two end points. Dress down to the lines with a file. If the steel resists,

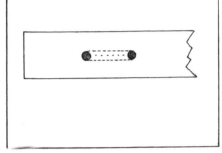

Draw or scribe connecting tangent lines as well as a center line for the slot.

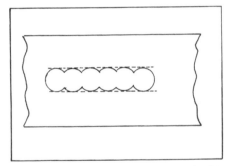

Bore the connecting holes. Clamps are absolutely necessary for this kind of boring. The drill will want to wander to the adjacent hole if the steel is not clamped.

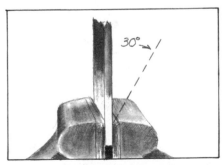

Set the curve in the cap iron. Although this can be done cold, heating the iron produces a cleaner, tighter curve.

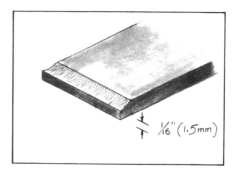

Establish the hollowgrind on the cutting iron.
Leave at least ¹/₁₆ inch (1.5 mm) of thickness for
the edge.

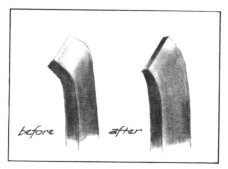

The iron on the left, just bent, is too thick and
abrupt, and needs refinement. The grinder and a
file will produce the desired results.

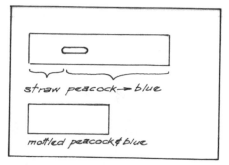

Temper the irons. Of the cutting iron, only the
area that may eventually be used as a cutting edge
is left at straw. The rest is blue. The cap iron,
because it will show in the plane, can be tempered
to peacock. A bright and striking mottle of purple
and blue, are a form of oxidization and lends
a slight amount of rust resistance to the steel.

particularly during boring, you may need to anneal again. Be sure to obtain the medium cherry heat and allow it to soak at that temperature before cooling slowly.

4. Bore the screw hole in the cap iron. Use the centerpunch to locate a hole site that is 2⅝ inches (66 mm) from the cutting edge end, centered in the width of the cap iron. If you are using a ¼ inch x 20 screw, use a No. 7 drill. If you elect to use another size screw, consult a chart to determine the right size hole to drill. Drill presses, drill indices, and giveaway posters usually have this information. Taking the usual precautions (clamps and backup board), drill the hole.

5. Set the curve in the cap iron. If you don't have the forge already lit, use the oxyacetylene torch to heat. Set the vise so that only one quick turn is necessary to lock the cap iron. (A little preparation helps ensure those necessary successes along the way.) Heat the last ¾ inch (19 mm) of the cutting edge end of the cap iron to orange, and lock about ½ inch (13 mm) of the heated end in the vise. This requires just light pressure; if you torque the vise handle with too much gusto, you will imprint the iron with the vise jaws. Pull back on the iron until it deflects about 1 inch (25 mm), or about 30 degrees from the perpendicular.

6. Establish the cutting edge on the blade iron. Leave at least ¹/₁₆ inch (2 mm) of thickness at the edge.

7. Dress the deflecting bend on the cap iron. The key to the cap iron's success is its perfect mating to the blade iron. The deflecter curve must meet the back of the blade exactly, precisely, without the hint of a gap. This work is best done with a file. Use even, balanced strokes. First, round the top of the iron. Do not thin it to less than ¹/₁₆ inch (2 mm), or you will lose the edge during hardening. After the top is rounded, flatten the inside edge of the deflector. (You will have to dress it again after hardening, but removing some of the thickness now will make it easier later.) Smooth all surfaces to 400-grit.

8. Harden the irons. Harden one iron at a time. Heat to a light cherry red and quench in oil, cutting edge first. Test for hardness with a file.

9. Clean, smooth, and polish. Even though it is fully hardened, smooth and polish the top of the cap iron. Use flap wheels and finish with 600-grit by hand. Not only will you use this side of the iron to read the temper colors, but you may want those colors to remain. Clean the back of the cap iron only to remove the quench oil. Flatten, smooth, and polish the back of the blade iron. Only the last 2 inches (50 mm) before the cutting edge is necessary for use, however, as this will be your window to tempering, it is necessary to polish the whole back. The other side of the blade, the bevel side, only needs flattening.

10. Temper the irons. Clean all surfaces with alcohol, naptha, or MEK. Even fingerprints will distort the colors. Temper the cap iron peacock to blue. Let the two colors mottle as it is attractive.

The blade must be more precise. The cutting edge and last 2 inches (50 mm) of the blade should be tempered to pale straw. The rest of the blade is divided half and half, peacock and blue. (Ideally, the pale straw would change immediately to blue. Running to peacock and then blue is easier and will result in a thoroughly serviceable blade.)

11. Tap the cap iron for the locking screw. Now that it is tempered, you will have no problem tapping the hole. Use even pressure and keep the tap perpendicular to the iron. If the tap feels as if it is beginning to bind, use a drop of oil on it and in the hole. Back out of the hole regularly to clear chips.

12. Fit the cap iron to the blade with the locking screw and washer.

13. Dress the cap iron. With the cap iron locked to the blade, observe the gap between the top edge

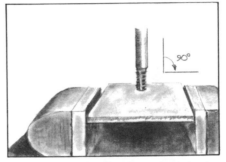

The trickiest part of making the cap iron is tapping the screw hole. Take the time necessary to ensure that the tap remains vertical to the iron.

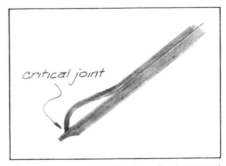

Fit the cap iron to the cutting iron. The juncture of the cap iron to the cutting iron must be tight. Any space between the two will allow shavings to get wedged in. Instead of curling shavings out of the throat of the plane, a poor joint will break the shavings and the plane will not clear itself properly.

A little extra pressure during honing will provide this slight rounding of the corners of the hollowgrind, exaggerated here for clarity.

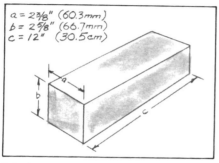

a = 2⅜" (60.3mm)
b = 2⅝" (66.7mm)
c = 12" (30.5cm)

Before making any cuts, the stock must be perfectly dressed. Failing to do so will result in subsequent cuts being off.

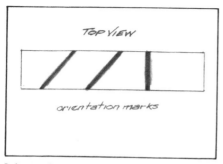

TOP VIEW

orientation marks

Before cutting the sides of the plane, mark what will be the top of the plane. This facilitates the reassembly and eliminates guessing.

of the cap iron and the blade iron. Calculate the angle in your mind. Demount the cap iron and, with a file, fair the inside edge of the cap iron. This may take a dozen tries. Be sure to tighten the cap iron to the blade each time you check it. If the iron is not fully tightened, the angle will be incorrect and there will be a gap. This is critical and well worth the time.

14. Complete the hollowgrind on the blade iron.

15. Sharpen and hone the iron. During honing, press harder at the corners of the blade. This will *slightly* round the blade and preclude the corners from digging.

PROCEDURE FOR THE PLANE BODY

1. Select materials. The wood type is not as important as the material's stability. Select wood that is dry and stable in your shop's atmosphere and has an even grain pattern. Burls or "squirrely" grain, even if located away from the sole, can still affect the plane. Finally, look for shakes and cracks. There are never any guarantees with wood, but in addition to checking all the exposed surfaces, try to predict how it will behave. Those smoky, brown-gray wisps of color in maple and beech are often indicative of cracks or shakes below.

2. Dress the body stock. This piece needs to be exactly square. Do not count on cutting away a defect or moving it to the outside; you invariably work your way into a corner with no exit. The body stock needs to be full-size and dressed square. If the body is to have a laminated sole, dress the stock after lamination.

3. Remove the plane sides from the body. Mark the stock as shown to help orient the pieces later. Using your best blade, cut ⅜-inch (10-mm) slabs from each side of the body on the table saw. Be sure the blade is square to the table, and do not hesitate during the cut. You will need the mating faces to be smooth. Have your push-stick in position and move the wood through the blade.

4. Cut the front and back sections of the throat. The bedding angle of the plane is 45 degrees. A motorized miter box is probably the perfect tool for this sort of cut. The table saw and miter gauge make me nervous when mitering such a relatively short and thick piece of stock. The 45-degree angle should exit the sole with 3 inches (80 mm) forward and 6 inches (160 mm) aft. (This ⅓:⅔ proportion seems to work best for most shorter planes.) To open the throat in the foresection, use the band saw. Scribe a sweep on the side of the block that will open the throat nearly perpendicular to the bed, and cut. (A straight cut of about 60 degrees would work, but I prefer a slight sweep.) Smooth, dress, and check both cuts. They *must* be square to the sides; if they aren't, recut them. This squareness is crucial. If the bed for the iron is not square, the blade will forever be skewed in the plane. If the foresection is off, the mouth of the plane will literally sneer and not maintain even pressure just in front of the cutting edge. As a result, the plane may dig, bite, or chatter. Check the squareness of the front and back sections with the plane sides clamped in position. Set them up on a flat surface. Line up the fore and aft sections of the mouth; its opening should be even.

5. Mortise the back section for the locking screw and washer. In order for the iron to rest flat and rigid against the bed, a channel has to be inlet for the width of the washer and the height of the screw head. A router table is the perfect tool for this; second choice is the mallet and chisel. After mortising the channel, check it with the blade to be sure there are no impediments to movement. The channel should be ¹/₁₆ inch (2 mm) wider than the washer to allow for lateral movement.

6. Drill holes for reference pins. By using dowels as reference pins, you can access the interior of

Cut the sides. Use a clean sharp blade with a steady even stroke. If you still get a burn, use a scraper to clean the surfaces. Sandpaper tends to round flat surfaces.

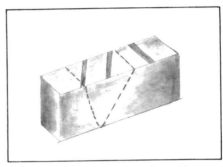

Use a miter box to cut the aft section at 45 degrees. The band saw, with the table perfectly vertical to the blade, will do well at cutting the forward slope.

Using a perfectly flat surface, check the alignment of what will become the mouth of the plane. It should be perpendicular to the sides and form a straight-sided opening.

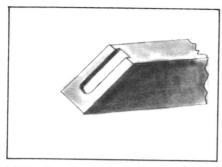

Inlet the aft section for the locking screw. Although a router will do the job, it's faster to use a chisel.

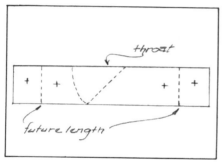

Lay out and mark the pinholes. Before boring the holes, be certain that the registration marks line up.

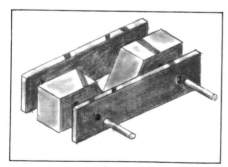

Before boring the inside pinholes, dry fit the assembly. Now is the time to check for any errors, before committing to the pins that will become a permanent part of the plane.

the plane for direct measurements and fitting. This makes it easier to locate the crossbar and trim it. The wedge can be made to fit precisely, and finally, of course, glue-up is easier because everything is aligned and held in place.

Locate and mark two pin sites for each section. One of each of those pins should be located in the last 1½ inches (40 mm) of either end. (These ends will be removed as waste after glue-up.) Line up the side slabs to mate the way you marked them, position the two inside sections so that the mouth is open 1/16 inch (2 mm), lock it all together with clamps, and check alignment. Use a backup board to prevent tearout at the hole exit. Bore holes ⅜ inch (10 mm) in diameter to match the pins. The body is now aligned with positive registration, and you still have access to the interior.

7. *Make, locate, and fit the crossbar.* With one side mounted to align everything and the other side removed to access the interior, position the blade irons on the bed as they will be during use. Position the wide face of the crossbar stock 5/16 inch (8 mm) from, and parallel to, the cap iron. Now move the crossbar up in the throat until the corner is ⅛ inch (3 mm) from the top edge of the side. Check again for the distance and the parallel faces. Use a pencil to outline the perimeter of the crossbar on the plane's side. Now draw the outlined rectangle's diagonals to locate the pivot pin site for the crossbar. Because you have used pins for alignment, you can now pin the two sides directly together and bore a single, perfectly aligned ⅜-inch (10-mm) hole without risking tearout. (A hole this size will match the body pins; it could be as small as ¼ inch (6 mm) and still be strong enough.) Carve round tenons on the ends of the crossbar to fit the holes. I use the table saw and the miter gauge with a stop to cut a square tenon that is a little larger than ⅜ inch (10 mm). Then I round it with a knife and file. The crossbar should be snug when in position, but it should be able to rotate. Check the crossbar by clamping the plane together with the bar in position. (A usual error is to leave the bar a little long, which prevents the sides from completely mating to the front and back sections.

8. Shape the wedge. Cut, sand, or plane the incline on the wedge so that it locks about ¼ inch (6 mm) above the deflector curve on the cap iron.

9. Glue up the body. Plastic resin glue is more rigid than the modified PVAs (yellow glues), and this is one application where the added drying time is worth the wait. Before mixing the glue, take the time to lay it all out in an organized sequence. Include clamps, rags, and water. Also take time to pencil a line around the front and back sections as they are silhouetted on the sides. This will help you to avoid spreading glue on the exposed surfaces of the throat. Remember to install the crossbar, but don't glue it. Clean all the obvious blobs of glue from the exterior, and use the rags and water to clean out the throat. Be sure that all joints line up flush.

10. Shape the collar. Don't think of the collar as an extension of the bed; it is intended as a handle. If you line up its 45-degree incline with the back section's bed, you make the construction more difficult than it needs to be. The collar can become a liability to proper seating of the iron. Plan on attaching it ¼ inch (6 mm) behind the back opening of the throat. Shape the collar to suit. Some students have taken time to carve this handle, resulting in handles with myriad tiny facets that made excellent gripping surfaces.

11. Shape and join the horn. The joint that holds the horn to the plane's body is a hidden sliding dovetail. While this may sound intimidating, using a router table makes it relatively simple. Before attempting to shape the horn, use the router table and a dovetail bit to cut the dovetail tenon. Stop the dovetail at 1¾ inch (45 mm) in length.

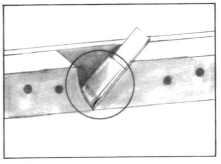

With all the holes bored and the pins holding one side of the plane in place, fit the iron. It should rest perfectly flat against the aft section. The cutting edge should not protrude. This is the time to make adjustments.

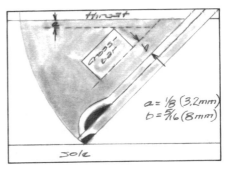

Locate the crossbar. Pencil marks for **a** and **b** will help.

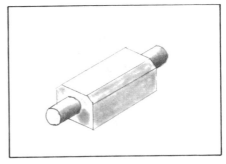

The shape of the crossbar is a matter of taste. Initials, dates, sometimes even scroll work are appropriate here. Most important, however, are the round tenons. They must be the same size and in line.

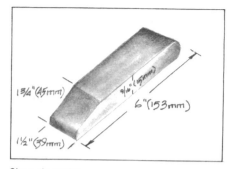

Shape the wedge.

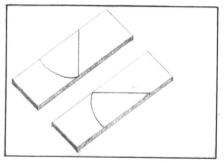

Marking what will be the throat on each side is important. The lines will indicate how far to spread the glue.

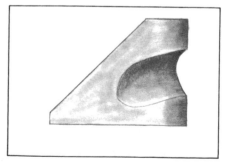

The collar ought to fit the shape of the craftsman's hand.

Adjust the tablesaw blade to the exact height of the shoulders of the dovetail, and make a crosscut at exactly 1¾ inches (45 mm) from the bottom of the block. This cut provides a smooth and even mating surface at the top of the plane. Shape the handle to suit.

12. Trim and shape the body. Flatten the sole first. Scrape and sand carefully. Everything should be square, so you want to avoid disrupting that. If you have a floor-model belt sander and are comfortable with it, you may want to use it to work the sole *lightly*. (You are not ready to open the mouth of the plane yet.) With the sole flat, smooth, and square to the sides, you can sand the protruding pins from one side and rip the other side clean on the table saw. A rip of ¹/₁₆ inch (2 mm) should be adequate to remove clamp and glue marks and other blemishes. Adjust the rip fence and rip the other side—again ¹/₁₆ inch (2 mm). Now that the sole and sides are flat and smooth, set the rip fence to remove ¹/₁₆ inch (2 mm) or so from the top of the plane. The long axis of the plane is now square. Mark the ends of the plane and crosscut it to finished length.

13. Adjust the mouth. I like to have ¹/₃₂ inch (1 mm) of opening forward of the cutting edge for a smooth plane. At this point, the blade iron should not protrude at all. You will need to dress down the sole by about ¹/₁₆ to ⅛ inch (2 to 3 mm) before it begins to press through. Begin by locking the irons in place with the wedge. Lock the wedge down as though you were going to use the tool. The idea is to stress and distort the plane as it will be stressed and distorted during use. I use a floor-model belt sander for dressing the sole. A large disc sander with an accurate table would work (at least to rough it down). Sandpaper on a flat machine table—though slow—is the most controlled method. (Do not use a table saw. Do not use the jointer. Both of these would have steel or carbide knives cutting within a hair's breadth of a piece of hardened steel. An error in judgment, a twitch, a cough—disaster.)

Whatever method you use, take your time. The mouth opens suddenly and you have only one safe shot at it. (If you do overshoot, inlay a piece of wood to refill the mouth. This also works to redress an old plane that has opened too much.) Be sure to shift your hand positions while working the sole. Switch the plane's orientation to the abrasive's direction as well. It will help to equalize the cut. Most important, frequently check the mouth's opening. If you are using power to sand, stop when the blade just protrudes. (Do not force the blade. This would be likely to tear out some of the sole just in front of the mouth. Again, the only solution is the inlay.) Sand that last bit to provide the 1/32-inch (1-mm) clearance by hand on the machine table. 180-grit is fine enough for this final sanding. The sole burnishes very quickly.

14. Cut the dovetail channel for the horn. Again, the router table seems to be the easiest approach. Use clamps and blocks to stabilize the relatively small surface of the plane's front end.

15. Locate and bore the rear collar pinholes. Drive two small tacks partway into the bottom of the collar, about 1 inch (25 mm) apart and ½ inch (13 mm) away from any edge. Snip all but 1/16 inch (2 mm) of the tacks off. Set the collar in position on the back end of the plane and press it down. You need to press just hard enough to mark the surface. You do not want to drive the tacks any deeper into the collar because you will need to remove them. Before you remove the tacks, be sure the marks are clear. Drill the holes in both pieces. (Use the stops on the drill press to avoid boring through the collar.) Cut the dowel pins to length, and test the fit.

16. Shape, sand, and finish the body. Soften the edges and do the final sand with 220-grit paper. Use tung oil for the finish—it has a nice feel. The first

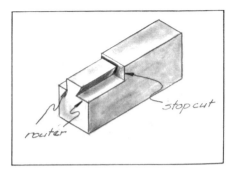

The sliding dovetail will make a strong invisible joint. The stop cut is necessary for the front tote to seat properly onto the front section of the plane.

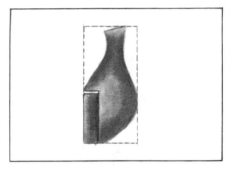

A traditional front tote. Like the collar, this is a custom piece and ought fit the hand of the craftsman.

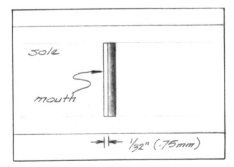

The mouth should be small on a smooth plane. The chip should not break until the last possible moment and a tight mouth will help to keep it down.

Using tacks to locate pinholes is an old but effective technique.

coat is 50 percent oil and 50 percent turpentine. The second coat is straight oil, which I rub out with pumice. Finish the rear collar and front horn also. Wait until the finish is applied, dried, and rubbed out before mounting them.

17. *Mount the handles.* Although I use yellow glue for the collar, I prefer hide glue for the horn. This makes it easier to remove a broken horn in the future, and the glue has more than adequate strength.

OTHER WOODEN PLANES

Making the smooth plane may seem difficult or terribly complicated. After a couple of successes, however, you will start thinking in terms of making other planes to your own specifications. By simply changing measurements, and perhaps the handles, a jointer plane is possible. Reshape the sole and blade and you have a scrub plane. Miniaturize and you make a carving plane. The possibilities are as great as your needs.

A Chariot Plane

There are many reasons for making tools: personal satisfaction; the increased utility of tools designed and made expressly for the craftsperson; the adventure of a new design or the pursuit of an old one that for some reason beckons and beguiles us. I had seen photos of this chariot plane. Done in brass with rosewood infill, it seemed so elegant. Even though the photos were in black and white, I could see the richness of the material. The design was subtle—a form following its function but without the noise of handles and other obvious distractions.

Though the critical climate is changing now, so much of the woodwork done on the West Coast has been dismissed as "California Roundover"—a propensity in the '60s and '70s to build a piece of furniture and soften it with a quarter-round bit and the router. I wanted to soften edges for my work, but not so soft nor mechanical as a router. The idea of a series of chamfering plane cuts occurred to me. It would provide more sinuous and touchable edge definition. And this happily coincided (of course) with my desire for a small chariot plane.

DESIGN

The sides of the plane are low in the front to accent the wooden infilled finger rest. The back of the finger rest is the forward face of the plane's throat. The sides of the plane rise to provide for a crossbar and subside again, revealing the wooden iron bed. The palm rest is also the wedge — a neat, economical design. This instrument, with its curves and planes, its wood and metal in pleasant juxtaposition, is beautiful. More important, however, the tool works.

I use the plane only for chamfering — for setting a radius of many small, overlapping cuts that result in an edge that is less formal, less mechanical than the router or shaper. The shape evolves and is guided more by hand and eye than predicted by the specifics of a particular bit.

The chariot plane is meant for one-handed use. Being made of metal, it is much heavier than a wooden plane of the same dimensions, but it is not too heavy. I used to use a block plane for this work, but it *was* too heavy. There was no sensing the cut. I have made similar designs in wood, but the requirements of the material changed the stream-lined shape and feel.

The bedding angle is different, too. Though 20 degrees may seem slight, this is a single-iron plane and the bevel faces up. This puts the actual cutting

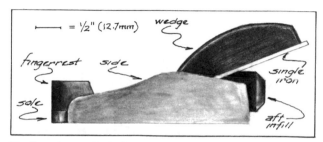

The dimensions of the chariot plane. Intended for one-hand use, the chariot plane is heavy enough to help reduce chatter and small enough to be used without fatigue.

angle at about 45 to 50 degrees. The angle seems appropriate in use.

MATERIALS

Brass	Brass lends itself well to this project. Not only are its color and texture warm and pleasant, but the metal also works very easily. Bronze is the second choice, but only because it can be much harder than brass. I have also made this plane from stainless steel, but the joints required special welding equipment and a lot of heavy filework.
Sides:	Two each of ⅛ x 1 x 3½ inches (3 x 25 x 95 mm).
Front Sole:	¼ x 1 x 2½ inches (6 x 25 x 65 mm).
Back Sole:	¼ x 1 x 1 inch (6 x 25 x 25 mm).
Crossbar:	¼ x ⅜ x 1 inch (6 x 10 x 25 mm).
Pins:	Ten each of 1/16 x ¼ inch (2 x 6 mm).
Steel	If you begin with smooth, flat stock such as old circular saw blades, knives, garden shear blades, and so forth, this tool can be made with only the torch.
Blade:	⅛ x ⅞ x 3¾ inch (3 x 22 x 100 mm).
Wood Infill	Rosewood and ebony were the typical infills for this sort of plane in the nineteenth century.
Finger rest:	⅝ x 1 x 1 inch (15 x 25 x 25 mm).
Bed:	⅞ x 1 x 2⅜ inch (22 x 25 x 60 mm).

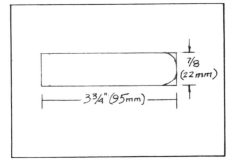

The single-iron dimensions.

PROCEDURE FOR THE BLADE

   1. Anneal the stock.

   2. Cut to shape. The key here is to keep the sides of the blade parallel. Scribe the shape and cut, grind, and smooth the outline. Flatten and smooth the front and back of the blade. Abrade to 400-grit.

   3. Establish the hollowgrind. Take the edge down to no less than 1/16 inch (2 mm).

After rounding the end, establish the hollowgrind. Leave it blunt to avoid burning during hardening.

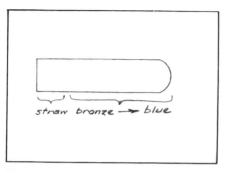

Although strictly speaking, the cutting edge should be straw and the back end of the blade blue, the transition between them may be bronze. This will lend a little stiffness to the single-iron blade, which would otherwise have a tendency to chatter.

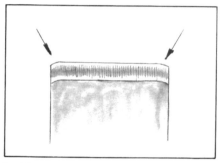

As with most plane irons, a slight rounding at the corners will reduce the occurrence of sharp-edged digs made during planing.

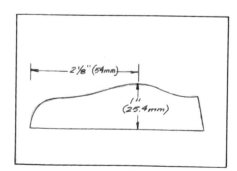

Silhouetting the sides is done with a jeweler's saw. Although slow, it is accurate.

4. Harden the blade. Heat to light cherry red and quench in oil, cutting edge first. File test for hardness. Clean, polish, and buff both sides of the blade.

5. Temper the blade. Clean all surfaces. Use soap and water or a solvent such as MEK. The temper colors should run from pale straw for the last ¾ inch (19 mm) of the cutting edge to blue for the rounded butt of the blade. I like to let the space between them mottle in peacock; there is very little stress on the blade's central section, and the peacock is lovely to look at. Unlike the smooth plane iron, this iron is easier to set if both sides are smooth, thus the extra work.

6. Finish the hollowgrind, sharpen, and hone. Remember to apply extra pressure at the corners during honing to give its width a hint of curve.

PROCEDURE FOR THE BODY

1. Silhouette the sides. If you get the brass stock from a supply house, do not have it cut to size by a shear. It will slightly distort the edges and make joining the pieces much more difficult. A hacksaw, a hand saw, or even a jigsaw (use beeswax on the blade) will work to silhouette the sides. For such small, delicate work, especially in brass, I like the jeweler's saw. Stay wide of the scribed line. You can fair the last 1/32 inch (1 mm) and smooth the curves with files. The straight bottoms of the sides are best kept straight by drawfiling.

2. Silhouette the sole sections. Because both pieces need to be exactly the same width, I usually start with a single piece, dress it, and then section it. Of course, this is not always possible. If you must work with two pieces, lock them together in a vise to dress the sides. If they are still not perfect, you will have a chance later to correct for most errors. The edges of the sole, however, must be perfectly square. These will be the surfaces of the butt joints that will be pinned and silver-soldered later. If they are canted, the sides of the plane will be canted. If they are irregular or rounded, the joints will be open and weak. If you have access to a disc sander with a solid and accurate table, use it to square the joints.

3. *Locate and drill the pinholes in the side plates.* Lay out the body pieces. Test their fit on a flat surface. If there is a little rocking in the sides because the sole pieces are uneven, you will have a chance to correct a small error. If the sides gap more than 1/32 inch (1 mm) you will need to work the sole sections again. Locate the soleplates where they will mate with the sides and mark the sides. Leave an opening of 3/16 inch (5 mm) between the front and back soleplates for the mouth. With a wood-marking gauge, scribe a *light* line 1/8 inch (3 mm) above the bottom edge of each side. Locate four sites for pinholes, two in the front section area and two in the back. Centerpunch them lightly; brass is much softer than the steel you have been working and so requires a lighter setting blow. Drill the holes (1/16 inch (2 mm) in diameter) through the plates. Just do the holes for one side of the plane at this point.

4. *Bore the back section for pins.* In order to bore the matching pinholes in the edges of the soleplates, you will need to make a simple jig. Rip a block of wood that is about 6 to 8 inches (150 to 200 mm) long to the exact width of the sole. Clamp the back sole section to it. Align the side to the sole section (using the marks from Step 3). The block should keep everything square and provide the necessary support for drilling. If you find it difficult to keep everything in alignment and drill the holes as well, a couple of dots of glue will help hold the side plate in position. Set the drill press for the correct depth, a little under 1/4 inch (6 mm), and bore the holes for the back section only.

5. *File the bedding level on the mouth side of the back soleplate.* Setting the bevel at this point is much easier than waiting until the plane is closed up. Scribe reference lines of 20 degrees on both

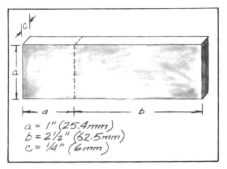

The sole dimensions. If cut from a single piece, the sides will be more likely to mate properly.

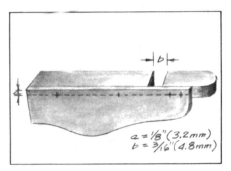

Use a wood-marking gauge and a light touch to lay out the pin line.

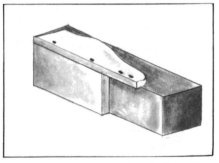

Use a block to support the side and sole together during boring.

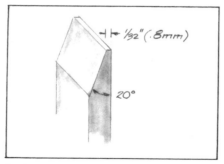

Set the taper on the back section soleplate. This incline needs to be absolutely flat since it is the support for the blade. If it is irregular or skewed, the blade will chatter.

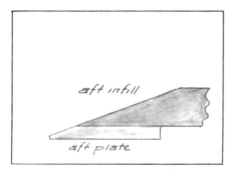

The aft infill should be as accurate as possible. Like the sole, this will support the blade when you are planing. If it isn't flat and true and set at 20 degrees, the blade will chatter.

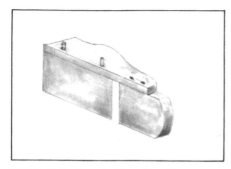

Set the aft pins for a dry fit-up. By setting one section at a time it is easier to insure accuracy.

sides of the forward edge of the soleplate. File an absolutely flat bevel. This bevel will be part of the iron's bed; if it isn't flat, the blade will not seat properly. Take the bevel down to $^{1}/_{32}$ inch (1 mm) at the edge. (The brass is too soft to hold a finer edge.)

6. *File a 60-degree bevel on the inside edge of the front soleplate.*

7. *Rough cut the wooden bed.* Now is the time, before anything is permanently set, to align bed, blade, and mouth. Cut the 20-degree angle on the back wooden infill. Don't worry about width or length now; the bedding angle should be smooth, clean, and accurate as well as flat.

8. *Pin the sides to the back section.* Line up the corresponding holes and insert the pins. Do not force the pins and do not set them. You will need to be able to disassemble for cleaning.

9. *Adjust the mouth opening and bore the pinholes in the front section of the sole.* This was your reason for using pins. Adjusting the exact opening of the mouth is much easier with the back section registered in position. You marked an opening of $^{3}/_{16}$ inch (5 mm) earlier to allow you to bore for the pins in the side. That $^{3}/_{16}$ inch (5 mm) is probably close, but you want it to be exact. Position the infill block so that the bedding incline is continuous. (Check it, too, for irregularities.) Take the finished blade and locate it on the bed. It should be positioned just as it will be during use, with the edge dropping just below the plane of the sole. Now line up the front section of the sole. You want an opening of $^{1}/_{32}$ inch (1 mm). Be sure that the sole is flush to the bottom of the side. Check the opening for evenness; if it's uneven, now is the time to adjust it. Mark the exact location of the front plate. Use a mark on the side piece at the mouth opening and on the soleplate where it extends beyond the side. Jig the assembly for drilling as you did before, and drill the pinholes.

10. *Prepare the joints for solder.* Joint preparation is the key to a good solder joint. Use 220-grit sandpaper with a hard, flat block to sand all mating surfaces. Even though they may not appear dirty or oxidized, you need to sand them. Something as slight as a fingerprint can disrupt the flow of the solder. Not until you have abraded the surface and been scrupulous about not touching those surfaces can you be sure that they are free of contamination. Sand carefully; you do not want to round anything over.

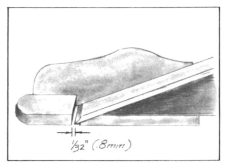
On a flat surface adjust the mouth, clamp, and drill.

11. Set the pins. These are small pins. Go lightly. Line up the holes, insert the pins, and tap gently. The holes are snug enough that a gentle tapping will upset and thicken the pins sufficiently to bite into the side and soleplates.

12. Solder the joints. Silver solder comes in three grades (hard, medium, and soft) and in two formats (wire and sheet). Use hard solder in a wire format. You will also want silver solder flux in a paste form. Spread the flux along the inside corner of the joint. A bead ⅛ inch (3 mm) thick should be adequate. Use something clean, other than your finger, to spread it. Do not flux the open area of the mouth. Cut two pieces of solder wire in the length of each joint. Straighten the wires and lay them on the flux. Again, avoid using your fingers directly.

Now you will need a soldering platform: something porous or nonconductive and fire-resistant. A charcoal block works well, as does a fire brick. Avoid using metal; it will serve as a heat sink and you will lose control of the process. A propane torch will provide all the heat you need. Place the assembly solder-side up on the platform so that gravity is holding the solder in place. You also need to be able to get to the joint with the torch flame from the bottom of the plane, so it should hang over the edge of the fire brick.

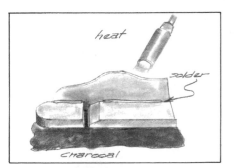
Be patient when soldering. Build the heat gradually. When the solder is ready, it will collapse suddenly and flow into the properly prepared joint.

Soldering is a relatively slow process. Make yourself comfortable. What you are going to do is heat the sole and side of the assembly to the same temperature at their joining surfaces. When the temperature is correct, the flux will bubble, vaporize, and remove any oxides on the brass. You heat the side opposite the solder and flux to draw them through the joint. As the temperature increases, the solder will flow. Obviously, how you heat is important. The sole is twice as thick as the sides, so more heat is required to bring it to temperature. Direct the flame so that its hottest point is about ⅛ inch (3 mm) onto the sole from the joint line. When the flux vaporizes, shift the flame directly to the joint line. After it has cooled—air cool, do not quench it—test the joint. It should be rigid. If the joint does not take, separate the pieces carefully (you will have to reclean and repin) and look at the joint surfaces. If the solder is adhering to the soleplates and not to the sides, more heat will be required on the sides. If the side plates took the solder, but the sole didn't, then the reverse applies. Adjust your heating accordingly. Try building the heat more slowly this time.

13. *Clean the interior of the plane and flatten the outer joint.* It is easier to clean up the discolorations left by soldering while the other side is off. This touch-up is only to remove superficial blemishes. This is also your second chance at lining up the outer edges of the two soleplates for joining. If it is not a flat joint, use the file or disc sander to flatten it. This is one of those little adjustments that allow the work to proceed. Just as in woodworking, most good work is a series of anticipations and adjustments that you make along the way.

14. *Bore the pinholes into the edge of the sole.* Line up the side plate with the two index marks you made, and bore the holes. Be sure the bottom is flush with the sole.

15. *Clean and prepare the joints for solder.* Follow the same procedure as in Step 8.

16. *Set the pins.* Remember, gentle taps.

17. Flux and solder.

18. Clean the interior joint line. Again, this is a cosmetic cleanup. You want to avoid altering the flat surfaces.

19. Cut and fit the crossbar. The crossbar needs to have a snug friction fit. Use a file to shorten it gradually. Keep the ends square.

20. Prepare the plane and crossbar for soldering. First locate the bar's position: 1½ inches (40 mm) back from the forward edge of the side. Flush the corners of the ends so that after soldering you can file the cross section of the bar flush to the sides. Mark the location with two lines on each side piece. Sand the mating surfaces to remove oxides.

21. Flux and solder the crossbar. As with the soldering of the sole, the flux and solder are positioned inside the plane. You apply the heat from the outside: more heat to the thicker section, the crossbar. Don't try to solder more than one side at a time.

22. Clean and smooth all the surfaces. The inside will be blemished again from the solder. Use some 220-grit to remove blemishes and 320-grit to polish the interior—everywhere. Use a small, flat piece of wood to support the abrasive. This is the last inside cleanup, and you want it to look pristine.

The exterior has some more significant cleanup to be done. The crossbar needs shaping with a file. Flush it to the curve of the sides. The sides will have discoloration and protruding pins. A floor-model belt or disc sander will rough it down; follow with progressively finer abrasives to suit your taste in finishes. If you want that golden mirror look, abrade to 600-grit (you will buff later). The bottom is probably not just discolored but has little buttons of hardened solder protruding as well. Place a piece of sandpaper on a hard, flat surface (a machine table), and with the sole down, describe

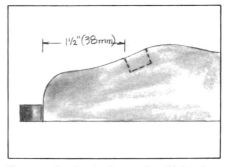

The proper location for the crossbar. If it is to be shaped, do so before it is soldered into position.

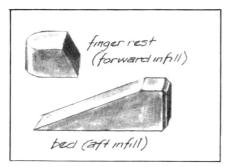

The infills are both functional and expressive.
Rosewood, ebony, or any number of other exotic
materials are appropriate.

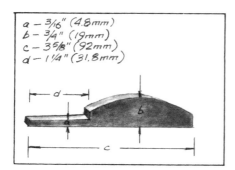

The wedge handle should fit the craftsman's
hand. Rounding, shaping, even carving the crest
can create the desired results.

figure eights with the plane. (If these solder buttons
are large, file them locally first.) Finish the sole at
320-grit.

23. Cut and install the infills. The bed and
finger rest need to be cut and smoothed to a snug
fit. Epoxy will lock the snug fit. Clean the metal
and wood mating surfaces with solvent (acetone or
MEK) prior to applying the epoxy. (Do not apply
finish to the wood before epoxying; the finish will
degrade the joint.)

24. Cut and fit the wedge. This requires the
most "fritzing." I like to fit up a trial wedge first and
scribe its shape to the actual stock. With the blade
in position, measure the distance between the
crossbar and the blade. Place a mark on the side of
the wedge that is 5/32 inch (4.5 mm) in from the
end. Move up 1¼ inches (30 mm), and mark the
height that you measured between the blade and
crossbar, adding 1/16 inch (2 mm). This height
should be about ¼ inch (6 mm). Connect the
marks and cut out the wedge on the band saw. Use
a file to make the final fit of the wedge. Keep the
surface flat. The wedge should lock into position at
about ¼ inch (6 mm) from the bevel. With a practice wedge completed, transfer its shape to your
infill stock. Scribe and cut; stay wide enough of the
line to allow for smoothing.

25. Finish the plane. The exterior brass surfaces
can be buffed if you want a mirror surface. It will
not stay that way with use, but it will age grace-
fully. Do not let the buffing wheel linger in any one
spot; keep the plane moving. Edges can lose their
crispness very quickly at the buffer. Use tung oil on
the wood.

Notes

Notes